I0525794

First published in la República Argentina as Mujeres al Borde de una
Palabra by Antonia Amprina. English translation prepared by Katie
Marguerite Gray

Work published within the framework of "Sur" Translation Support
Program of the Ministry of Foreign Affairs and Worship of the Argentine
Republic. Www.programa-sur.mrecic.gov.ar/

Obra editada en el marco del Programa "Sur" de Apoyo a las Traduc-
ciones del Ministerio de Relaciones Exteriores y Culto de la República
Argentina. See Article 12 of the Rules for the SUR Translation Support
Program at: Www.programa-sur.mrecic.gov.ar/

Library of Congress Cataloguing in Publication Data

Words of Fire! Women Loving Women in Latin America

ISBN: 978-0-9982521-0-0

Jordan Madere@jordan_tattoo

Words of Fire!

TRANSGRESS·PRESS

Words of Fire!

WOMEN LOVING WOMEN IN LATIN AMERICA

Antonia Amprino

Translated by
Katie Marguerite Gray

Translator's Note

The English version of this book is the realization of a personal desire of mine. *Mujeres al Borde de una Palabra* is a book that found its way to me while I was traveling in Argentina at the age of twenty in 2011. Having been through some trying situations in relation to my family and my own confidence as a lesbian, I had been thinking of writing a book to delve into the psyches of those labeled sexual minorities. I was at the beach for a solo trip when I met a couple who took me in as their weekend companion. Andrea recommended that I read a book written by a friend of hers, Antonia Amprino. When I returned to Buenos Aires I searched for the book and I devoured it on a twenty-one hour bus ride across Argentina to Chile. I wrote in the margins and underlined quotes and language. I remember the terminology being difficult for me because I was unfamiliar with it. Not only in Spanish, but I had never read lesbian literature before, even in English. But I remember relating to some of the stories and being taken aback by some others. Some ideas in the book were contrary to mine. Some of the opinions were offensive to me, but the book showed dialogue. It showed acceptance. It brought together the voices of many women to create a colorful web of imagery and life.

When I found this book again during a move two years ago, I re-read it. As I read the stories I remembered what the book had meant to me and I wished to share it with other women in my life. In an ambitious moment I decided to translate it for them. So I contacted Antonia and after some conversations Antonia allowed me to start the project. We worked closely. She reviewed my first pieces translated and then we went in search of finding a grant and an editor. The editor was an enthusiastic voice and strong supporter of the project. He challenged me all the way through. The grant came from the Argentinian government. How proud we are of that! Antonia went to the capital and presented the project in person. I received a tearful voice message from her when we were notified that we received the grant. She told me it was in that moment she realized we really had something here and that for the first time she was truly emotional about it.

As the project is now finished I am relieved. Although it has all come together in under two years, it has still been a challenge, arduous at times, and also a pure joy to complete. I loved working with Antonia and her constant support and faith in my skill and drive.

As far as my relationship with the book, the first time I read it was for my own sanity, partly due to my personal struggles with my religious family, their conservative values, the shame and the silence. It was a step I took in the direction of being more open about my sexuality, not only in public but with anyone in any place. Because of how I grew up, I was trained to make up stories, live a double life and hide. This book helped me to see that many women live that way and the women interviewed expressed such relief when they stopped hiding. The book helped me to say "Hey, this is me. I will not be held back by anyone else." Soon after my time abroad, I came out to my mom for a second time, this time to say, "It never went away. I am still gay."

Years later, reading the book again, I picked up on different details. My Spanish is now fluent so that I understood the underlying messages and little comments throughout. At this point in my life I am noticing some scarring and baggage left from the way I managed my sexuality as an adolescent, my own reactions to the external and internal pressures. This certainly affects amorous relationships, the way I communicate (or don't), the way I speak, the way I carry myself, dress, love, the way I open myself or close off, and when I commit or quit. Reading the words of these women here, I see similar stresses. It is quite interesting that each woman has some scar or difficulty, something that she had to overcome emotionally which almost always affected one or more serious relationship.

Therefore, my conclusion is that sharing stories is extremely important. Discovering that other women have had the experiences you have had or have thought the same thoughts you are thinking, even knowing that other women who are also gay see it differently, sheds a new light on who we are as a community. Communication in a personal sense is not my strong suit; it is what I am now facing and working through with help from friends and support networks. As I have now taken two very distinct journeys with this book, I cannot wait to see what I discover about myself when I read the book again!

Another reason for choosing this text is because of the cultural content. Translating it to English will allow the Argentinian, the Latin

American culture, language[1] and ideology to be shared with English speaking readers. The comparisons that you will draw with your own culture are sometimes striking, sometimes subtle. You will start to notice the role that culture and society play on how we handle, understand, and live our sexuality.

This book is dedicated to lesbian and bisexual women in hopes that the voices you find here will touch you, each in a unique way, as they did me. And to all of those who do not know where to start in understanding their sexuality, I hope that this book may bring some comfort and relief and that you may find peace.

Enjoy this book, enjoy these stories, and enjoy the journey that Antonia so aptly takes you on, guiding you through the life of each woman and adding her flare throughout. Most of all, be happy in who you are, be well, and share your troubles and successes. Find a group, a friend, find support, and do not be afraid to share. Knowing others' experiences may help you escape your struggles sooner and less painfully. For us all.

Katie Marguerite Gray

---

1 The following Spanish terms are used throughout this book: *tortillera* for dyke, *tortita* for lipstick lesbian or femme, *torta* for gay, and *marimacho* for butch. *Torta* literally means cake.

Author's Note

To write a book is to begin a journey as we have the vehicle and the destination. It is the result of patience and moment after moment looking for information and in my case, sifting through interviews. Sitting in front of a computer screen for hours upon end, sometimes just watching the continuous blinking of the cursor line which pollutes the rest of the blank page. Then, just as I feel that the page will never be filled, the cursor begins to move and letters appear, soon joining together to form words, then phrases, finally paragraphs. As I begin to feel the flow and more letters and words follow, the phone rings and distracts me, or I hear the ding of a Facebook chat message. Then the cat begins to meow asking for food and jumps onto my desk leaving a ball of fur on my keyboard, completely uninterested in my desire to continue with my inspiration.

This is more or less what happens when I write, but something very different happened when my writing was translated to English.

At first I was filled with various sensations and feelings: pride, surprise, even doubt. Would she be able to capture the story I was trying to say and tell?

Then began my interaction with the translator and soon I felt again satisfaction which proved to me that books are the children we give birth to. They are free and have their own journey. This, my first child, has had quite a long journey already.

We agreed on this project and began searching for funds to pay for the English edition which took us much time and effort. But it was successful and we are happy in this final stage.

Soon after, I was receiving almost daily messages through WhatsApp or by email. What do you mean to say with this phrase? Explain to me, please, what you mean by *tortillera?* And from there an endless stream of questions. Each one led me into a re-reading of the book, in a way. I began to rethink what I had published, to question the phrases, the details I relayed and even my own coming out story. I realized that possibly I could have left out all the details I included about that. But knowing that I have changed since then does not make me regret what I have created.

The time to translate the book was almost a record as our enthusiasm accelerated our process to create and Katie dedicated her time and all her talent. And so we continued with the work of translating these words.

The time has come to think about presentations and currently we are designing this new adventure inside the larger one, to be able to carry with us the voices of all the women who are included in *Mujeres al Borde de una Palabra*. We are hopeful that these voices will resonate in many women, regardless of country of origin.

In the middle of all of this there was the attack in Orlando. We were shocked and saddened, as was the rest of the world. We could not believe such cruelty, anger and hate. And once again we feel vulnerable along with the rest of the LGBT community.

Today July 14, 2016 is a month after this terrible event and we believe that it is a valiant effort to not hide and silence ourselves, to continue the work to be visible every day, each moment, so that the new wave will be life and not death.

We will travel with these words transformed into fire, alive with the warmth of other women who tell us all that we exist, that we live, and that we have the right to join together as we are—that this fact is not rebellion but passion, the pulse of life. It does not matter what language we write or speak in. The rights we declare should be the same from here to China. See you soon!!!!

Lic Antonia Amprino

Contents

Introduction

Words of Fire! Women Loving Women in Latin America is a compilation of stories of women who had the courage to step out of heteronormativity and take a leap from this realm of invisibility that says romantic relationships and couples must be established with the opposite sex. These are stories that lie outside of society's established norms. But this does not make them bad or wicked, although sometimes judged as such. Many of us who told our experiences in these pages found ourselves in a particular moment in life, in love with or attracted to another woman or other women.

Some women left the realm of heterosexuality and never returned. Others move fluidly back and forth between heterosexuality to homosexuality. Freely loving, they fall in love with the person and not the gender of the person.

This book is the result of many intense conversations conducted in chat rooms and in person with women who called themselves lesbian, gay, or bisexual. It grew out of my curiosity to know how other women approach what can sometimes feel like an abyss—the experience of loving another woman. Yet these women still allow themselves to live the life they feel, giving themselves permission to leave the heteronormative gender binary. This is also the story of how women have continued to define themselves, searching for and sometimes integrating an identity which was ignited by their love of a woman.

It is not an easy task for many women to recognize themselves as lesbian or bisexual in a world where the majority of the people living in it are heterosexual and where, many times, the choices that escape this definition are classified as perverted, indecent or abnormal.

Compiling different stories from interviews with women who were able to come out of the closet influenced my work. This is my response to compulsory heterosexuality. I wanted to contribute to a space for women who remain anonymous in their heterosexual lives, conforming to the norms which have been instilled in us since childhood. For example "Women wash the dishes and men work in the field." "Girls dress in pink and boys dress in blue." "Women do not sit with their legs apart." "Boys don`t cry." These are a few of the ingrained ideas that determine our daily actions and behavior, constructing who we are.

Each unique story comes together in this book to contribute a drop in the bucket for the readers. Whether they be heterosexuals, lesbians, men or women, each reader can in some way or another approach the day-to-day lives of the women who are included here with their stories, feelings and manner of constructing themselves differently. With their voices they interrupt the linear, heterosexual discourse. With their emotions they break the chains that bind us and box us in.

Words of Fire! contains the transcribed interviews chosen by the author along with her analysis of their meaning and value. The author's hypothesis is that naming ourselves is the first step to becoming free and that the words we use are important. She orders the interviews based on her arguments throughout the text. This book is a humble contribution to change the public's perception of lesbians and of women choosing different romantic and sexual partners. It offers a view into the lesbian world without intending to be a manual or establishing scientific conclusions.

CHAPTER ONE
Come Out of the Closet:
How to Be Heterosexual and Die Trying

How difficult it is to tell one's own story. I think this is partly because of our fear that what happens to us will hardly be important to other people. Courage is necessary, any amount that remains, and it comes from the desire we all have to be heard, to be listened to and to share our hopes and dreams. I will share my coming out of the "closet" story with you and what this meant for me and for my family. Of course they're included because that is what it means to come out of the closet: that your most intimate circle learns that being a man you like men and that being a woman you are interested in women.

Today when I look back I feel that I lived part of my life in ignorance and as an idiot, but as the band *Callejeros* says—"That which stays repressed, sooner or later tends to come out." You may agree also that: "Every action will receive its due reply."[1] The expression in Spanish is credited to San Martin. There is no escape, finally, from confronting who one is. Without a doubt you and I are going to go where we want to arrive, not anywhere else.

My coming out was a little more than five years ago when I took a vacation. As always on vacation, I felt unleashed, and why not say it,

---

1 This adage *"a todo chancho le llega su Sanmartin" refers to a national hero in Argentina and also the name for the tool that's used to slaughter pigs.*

rowdy and free of any worry. With the beach and the sand, (sucundun, sucundun)[2] and a beautiful and persistent woman, who slowly but unapologetically began a courtship. She teased me ("she pulled at my wing" as they say in my town)[3]. A little bit astonished I asked myself, why does she say this to me? Is she only toying with me or getting closer to me? But then after flirting with me she did nothing else but talk incessantly about men and her sexual experiences with them.

I want to clarify for you that until that moment I had not imagined being with a woman, that is to say having sex with a woman, making love passionately. If at some point I had thought of it, the sexual part gave me such disgust only to think of it.

But with the passing of time, I recognized it was a passionate nonsexual relationship with the friend of a friend—a fascination of one with another, and vice versa. She was enraptured listening to me talk and sharing personal feelings while I was enraptured with all of her, with her gaze, with her long skirts, the movement of her hips, her newscaster voice. Well, long story short, it ended with her accusing me to her friend (our friend in common): "Your friend is gay," and she sent me an email saying more or less: "Do not send me more emails, do not call me and do not come over to my apartment anymore." Obviously, I did not understand her reaction at all. I asked myself almost every day, "What did I do? What happened to her?"

My friends noted the consternation that I felt after that and being my friends, one of them dared to tell me: "Look, so-and-so is saying that you are homosexual." Obviously I denied it intensely. "That's crazy!!!!!" I denied it from an unconscious place, from the only place I knew, that is to say, "Boys have to go out with girls and vice versa," without the possibility of romantic or sexual encounters with others of the same sex, because it is not possible in our culture. It is actually quite impossible, or at least it was before.

Undoubtedly this was the theme of my next therapy session and I innocently excused myself saying, "The only thing I did was react to a stimulus. I do not know why she said that." My therapist said to me with finesse, "Are you listening to yourself?" Here the question is not if she is homosexual; it is if you repress your sentiments or not. What is at issue here is whether or not you are a lesbian."

At that moment I could not accept myself, I did not have the courage

2 Song reference
3 *"te arrastra el ala"*

4

to confront all that I needed to confront. In other words I did not have the ovaries to do so. But the important thing is that there is always a second chance.

When my coworker suggested a party, an "anything goes" kind of party (to clarify, she meant girls with girls and sexual high jinks) the coward inside me returned center-stage. But soon, like thin layers of an onion that fall one at a time to leave the center of the heart revealed, my mask fell away. My essence was exposed: vibrant, restless, anxious, disrupted, nascent—a pure metamorphosis. I felt as if I were another of Kafka's beetles! Here in front of me was an immanent change on the horizon and a struggle within myself. I felt as if I were upside down fighting with tremendous desperation to turn over and flip myself back up!

The party my coworker had suggested was nothing more than a trio; we had sex and now, after five years, I accepted it because I wanted to give myself liberty to make love to a woman. But as it was in the presence of a man who instigated it, who defined in some way the roles, it was not an act of purely homosexual pleasure or sex. It was a game established so that both of us brought pleasure to him. I do not deny that it was one of the most important and pleasurable sexual experiences of my life, but today I am certain that it was not the best.

After this experience that would be labeled bisexual, almost immediately after came love, with no third party or man around. This time it was an entirely homosexual encounter (surprising to me at the time). My relationship was with another co-worker. She was not a local coworker; she worked in another sector in Buenos Aires. We met through the company's intranet in the literature forum where we both wrote some poetry and posted texts from other authors.

At the beginning we communicated from a distance as coworker-friends who were happy to share readings and comment on books, with almost daily contact through technology.

Everything changed on the 8th of March when she sent me an email to my personal work email, a greeting for Women's Day and a message which was something like "Cheers to us, simply for being women." To which I responded (without filter or tact), "I agree with you vaginally." Obviously she was taken aback and the email was not answered immediately as she pondered my response. The emails continued and we jumped headlong into an intense friendship. During that time I was also close to some gay friends who were a couple. At the beginning I did not want to tell them that I was attracted to this woman who lived many miles away and whom I had never met. I did not want to tell them because I feared being boxed and labeled because I also had many doubts about my feelings and desires.

Obviously the attraction for this girl became something more; the desire to meet her continued growing with every email I received. I felt a tickle in my stomach and I must confess that I went to work at the company at that time with some desires that were unusual for me.

Then everything happened suddenly. She called me at my house. I had asked her once if she had been to the city of Rosario and invited her to come. Well, she said she would come that weekend. Rosario and the capital, Buenos Aires, are both in Eastern Argentina, the capital being on the Atlantic coast and Rosario about 200 miles inland to the west.

It was Wednesday when she told me she would come. Two seemingly endless days separated us. I began to talk to my gay friend's boyfriend to tell him about the anxiety I was feeling about meeting this woman, to say for the first time that I felt attracted to someone of the same sex.

I felt a volcano about to erupt of newly discovered passions inside me, feelings of complete freedom mixed with self-judgment and sentiments of guilt. I also experienced many fantasies that were growing each day and a rush of questions to which I could not find answers.

But nothing mattered to me except to meet this woman who fed my fantasies. She was my lighthouse at that time. And I had set my mind on this, although for a few moments the idea crossed my mind to call her and tell her not to come. Wimp? Yes! I had never felt weaker in my life, but I did not really know at the time what I was afraid of. Now that time has passed, I can say it was the fear that I would like being with her *a lot*. And that was it. I saw her get off the bus and immediately I knew that it was her. Her smile was a light that said, "It is me."

And there we were standing at the platform number 4 at 11 p.m. on March 22, with clear signs of anxiousness, with our own anxiety of seeing each other for the first time. All the emails that we had sent now had faces, smiles and gestures.

We did not stop looking at each other. Sometimes I tried to move away. I stayed some two inches from her to see her, and then I returned to her side to smell how her perfume invaded my senses, how the sound of her laugh intoxicated me.

I could have stayed for hours looking at her mouth since before we had our first kiss I was sure how those plump lips would feel. I imagined the moistness of her tongue restlessly fighting with mine. I felt how the fire began to cover our bodies little-by-little but spread with intensity.

From the first moment we saw each other we talked all night, we recognized each other, we realized that each word spoken had been pure and truthful, that we had been honest the whole time. I kept coming back to a question that I did not want to ask, that which I held back for fear that it would ruin everything, that I was wrong. I feared discovering that my assessment of the relationship had been a misunderstanding, that I had poorly interpreted the situation. I feared that she would also escape and the situation would turn out to be like the first woman I had been infatuated with.

At that moment in the night I wanted to try those lips, bite them, feel them, imprison them and put myself little by little into her mouth. I wanted her to be the place in the world to spend my life.

My desires to kiss her grew together with my doubts and I asked myself, was she feeling the same desire that I was? I asked the question; I do not remember today exactly how I formulated it. At first her reaction was to look at me surprised and later tell me, no, I do not go out with women.

My surprise was greater. I was somewhat perplexed and I went to the bathroom. When I returned she was sitting in the spot where I had been sitting. I asked her what had happened, why she was sitting there now and she lowered her eyes as a response. I came closer. I understood that it was not the time for words. I took her face in my hands and placed my lips on hers and little by little we shared our lips in a penetrating kiss. Later we moved apart to look at each other only to return to the taste of each other's skin, to recognize each other's moistness, know each other's excitement.

The first night of love we slept spooning, in an unending hug, celebrating having found each other. With the security of knowing that in the morning she would be there to wake up with kisses, hugs and cuddling.

Our love was short, but intense. The physical distance that separated us was dissipated by chats and phone calls. We saw each other every weekend and we did not stop loving each other. We spent all of our time in bed while time was nipping at our heels. We ran through the streets of Rosario free and happy, she much freer than I.

That was life then: wait for her and enjoy her when she arrived, know her closely, even with the distance, and dream of her until she came back to sleep with me.

The goodbyes, when it was time for them, were sad. We stood on the platform, avoiding contact, and feeling that people were watching us. We avoided giving the kisses that we desired, wanting to make out like a couple that needs the last kisses to survive the distance. For both of us it was our first experience; we shared the same fears, the same feelings of self-discovery.

Maybe for this reason we were startled and could not stay together in this love which began to give way to heartbreak.

And life continued on for me, in sort of a meaningless, non-descript way and I felt it in my body like a small dagger in my throat. And I found myself feeling a pain that I could not share with my friends.

At that time I had a heart broken by a woman. But despite my pain I felt at least some of my experience had been clarified.

The first and almost fundamental realization was that I liked women and that I chose to date women, that making love to a woman was beautiful. I came to heed what Juan Pablo Geretto[4] had told me years before, "You have to try a clam." To me this meant to be free and express what I felt. I wanted to live my life with dignity and without hypocrisy. I had been afraid to say, "I like women," and to feel the abyss that I had felt for a long time. I came to the conclusion I could not and did not want to continue living a lie.

I knew that it was not going to be easy for me or for my family either, but I wanted to share the fact that I was gay with others. It was a necessity that started slowly, but with incredible force. First I began to tell my closest friends. They all reacted well, no one was horrified and even a few of them said, "Finally you decided!" "Was it that obvious?" I would ask, to rid myself a little of the distress that was caused from accepting that I was attracted to a woman.

At the moment when I defined myself I also had to fight against some personal judgments, those which told me that in order to like women I had to be masculine, what the gay culture calls *marimacho or camionera*. I

---

4 Argentinian actor and friend of the author.

understood that some women identified like that, but I did not. And so the difficult part of fully defining myself remained.

Christmas dinner was very sad indeed because days before my father had died. My brother, the middle one, as always, looked at me cruelly, saying, "*Torta*." I looked him in the eyes and said, "Yes, you're right." I think everyone choked on their food, my mother feigned to have misunderstood and my sister stared at me with eyes like two daggers. The dinner continued as best it could and no one spoke more on the topic at least that night. The next day my sister said that I was a liar, that I was lying, that it was not true what I had said the previous night. I told her that yes, it was true, that I was a lesbian, and that the girl with whom I spent much of my free time was my girl. Of course she criminalized me for being proud of who I was and how could it be, that my mother was going to suffer with this decision and that I could have and should have waited a few years to come out, because my mother was old and sooner or later would die. That is to say that, plain and simple, I should put my life on hold in the service of what she thought was best for everyone else despite the fact this was obviously not what was best for me. But I felt that she did not care about what was best for me. In that conversation I realized I was able to say that I was proud because I allowed myself to live who I was, proud to be able to share my identity. I knew that I must embrace who I was and validate myself in order to withstand certain violent and discriminatory comments which could be heard from all sides. I was happy even though some reactions from my family were troublesome. Regarding my brother who always made fun of me, I must say that I silenced him forever. Never again did my brother bother me about being gay. I believe that we must put limits on people so that they do not take advantage of us or continue to hurt those who cannot or do not defend themselves. One year later I spoke directly with my mother who said that she did not understand because I was a woman so I explained, "Yes, Mama, I am still a woman, but one who chooses another woman to love. I will not change in any other way. I am still your daughter with all of my defects and maybe for you this decision is one more defect. I know that it will be difficult for you to understand and accept, but it is what I choose for my life. I am sorry that this hurts you so much."

I can tell you, as a final reflection that I am happy, not all the time of course, only idiots can be happy all of the time. In a major way your happiness depends on the decisions that you make in life and some choices are more difficult than others. Homosexuality is something that will cost you a lot no matter if you believe it is chosen or a gift. Either way your happiness depends on you allowing yourself to define yourself. My hope for you is that your family and friends will accept you as you are and will continue to love you. Finally, let us be free and less hypocritical.

And let us convince our heterosexual male friends to be gay so that we can keep all of the women for ourselves!

CHAPTER TWO

The Husband, the White House, and the Yellow Dog

The first conversation where I talked about this book took place in my home at a get-together with friends who came over for pizza and beer.

This conversation happened unplanned, but as it is at almost any gathering of friends or recently acquainted women, the question, "Hey, when did you realize you were gay?" came up. It is the magic question, the moment when everyone shuts up for a moment and listens to whoever has the floor. It seems that everyone soon starts to theorize, draw conclusions and place their personal story into the one being told, inevitably looking for similarities between the story being told and their own experience. The result is to almost always arrive at the same conclusion, *Of course, how could I not be a torta?!*

There were a few of us at this gathering and the one who first began to tell the story of her self-definition had been very involved in religious practices. Her sexual awakening happened during a retreat of the religious organization to which she belonged. At first she allowed this encounter with another woman who seduced her to take place, but then the guilt became too much and they ended up confessing what happened to the president of the mission. They felt the need to look to others for permission r condemnation for what had happened. And they looked to the very person who represented the law and the rules. They looked for

11

a nod of approval or disapproval with the intention of categorizing and naming the sensations and feelings which until that moment could not be described or named.

The formerly religious woman began her story, "My first experience was with a friend at the mission. The experience was important because what we had always thought and believed fell apart. I remember that we spoke with the president of the mission who made a crude drawing of me wearing a little skirt. Then he said, 'This is you,' (pointing with arrows) indicating I had changed direction and was now going to Hell."

The woman continued, "We told him everything in detail because we wanted to do what was right and because we did not understand what was going on with us."

The homosexual awakening that erupts within the confines of a person's religious life and beliefs disrupts that regimentation and control that is normally a part of every religion.

The telling of their experience, for these girls, was a way to avoid choice: the choosing of a romantic partner against the norm. It was their attempt to cleanse themselves of this act through words and return to the designated heteronormative plan. My friend continued, "After that I lost much of my faith in God and in any kind of "perfect plan," because at that moment I was balancing my life and I did not know in which direction I would turn."

As we listened, it was obvious that the woman was angry so I asked,

"With whom are you angry?"

"Angry with God," she said. "I imagined that there was a face behind a cloth and that the face was laughing. It was grim for me, because really I suffered a lot. And when I realized that I had lost that unconditional faith in God's perfect plan, it seemed like a very bad joke. I felt humiliated to have to speak with the president of the mission and to have to tell him everything. I also felt that there was so much hypocrisy because they had forgiven me but I was not repentant for anything. I gave a superhuman effort to do what they had asked me to do, but I was not sorry in my heart. I did not regret anything I had done. I was "clean again" according to their rules, for their sake, so I could return to do all the super-sacred things that only immaculate, saintly people do. I realized that it was all a lie. And when I realized that I had lost my faith I stopped going to church and I stopped following the strict practices that the religion demanded. Even though I was no longer in a romantic relationship with the woman I had loved, we stayed in contact. Our relationship had not ended but I was confused. We knew that we wanted each other but we did not know how to continue.

At first we had the idea that we could rise above what had happened and continue as friends. But she told me that it upset her and we stopped seeing each other. I felt that I would die with the distance and at one point I thought that I had to do something, call her to see how she was doing, to speak with her. Then another girl from the mission called me to tell me that she, my first love, was going to marry. We stopped talking in October and in December she married, it seemed to me, the first guy to come along."

As our get-together of women proceeded, the other participants made comments,

"What balls you had to admit what happened to the mission president." Obviously the question was, "Why did one woman decide to leave the religious life while the other not only continued in the religion, but even got married and committed to that lifestyle?"

"I knew," the woman responded, "that my girlfriend was going to do something like that, that she was going to do something rash, that she would do anything to forget herself and to end up with the husband, the white house, and the yellow dog."

The motives could be various and we only have vague answers to give, or maybe a lukewarm attempt to explain the behaviors.

"I think," she said, explaining the conduct of the other girl, "that it has to do with her surroundings. She was immersed in a very strict religious atmosphere where she felt a need to be accepted. Her whole life was turned upside down. It was easier for her to conform."

One question began to appear in the talk: "More than knowing what you are and what you feel, do you feel the need to say, 'I am a lesbian, I am *torta*'?"

Another participant answered yes and said, "I think that hearing yourself say it is when you reaffirm your sexuality and afterward you repeat it to give yourself strength and courage to confront what will come next." She added, "Hearing other women's stories helps you to understand that there are different situations. There are those of us who say I am going to try this and see if this is where my happiness lies and where I feel truly whole and then there are those who try to hide what they know and live as if everything is satisfactory when it's not."

I took this opportunity to ask the second woman: "When did you figure it out, or when did you start to ask yourself if you liked women?"

"When I came to the city of Rosario and saw."

"What did you see?"

"I saw that this exists, women in love with women."

"Before that, lesbians did not exist for you?"

"That's why I said that in Rosario, the love of women got my attention. Experiencing this freedom in Rosario made the possibility of loving another woman real for me. Before Rosario, I did not even ask myself to think of the possibility of liking a woman, but yes, now it makes me think. I can tell you that I looked for friends in women, not in men. Now I know that there was attraction. Before, I either envied women or hated them but in reality it was pure attraction. Now I see loving women as more natural. And now society affirms it, too, again and again, that there are women loving other women; it is more visible. This was reassuring because in my own town, it was not that way.

"In my town it was far worse. I escaped to be a lesbian somewhere else."

"But look at how crazy that is," another responded, "In my town I did not even realize lesbians existed but now I return, I pay attention, I realize that yes, they exist and even more, they were always there, suffering in a miserable silence."

"Exactly. So perhaps you did not have your radar on. Are they young or older lesbians?"

One of the women answered again. "No, they are older lesbians. I discovered later. I had been analyzing other ways to be happy with someone or something. And I gave myself the opportunity to try this type of love and I stayed."

"And you said, 'Wow, how wonderful this is!'"

"I stayed here," she explained, "but that came after some time. It was hard for me to accept myself. I spent a year in depression and self-discovery."

"By self-discovery, do you mean masturbation?"

"No, in my case it was emotional self-discovery. I was really quite depressed by not having found someone. I had found one person whom I truly loved and I knew that she also liked me a lot. When I could not be with her I felt terrible and I became depressed."

"Are you referring to the girl from the mission?"

"Yes, and also to begin from zero in every way. I went back after two years in complete crisis. I did not even have clothes that fit because I had gained so much weight from the depression and all of the stress. But I continued accepting myself, little-by-little, and I think I only stayed alive because of my responsibility to get up and go to work. I erased everything and started over to begin to live again."

Another woman asked, "And what happened when you had your second real sexual experience with a woman?" (Somehow this woman felt offended by the question and tried to escape by saying, "You are not the one asking the questions.") I intervened by clarifying that the format for our conversations was intended to be an open discussion and any question was permitted by any of the participants.

She continued,

"Well, really when I said 'This is who I am', I accepted it and began to digest it. I said, "Ok, let me see what there is out there."

"Yeah, whatever happens, happens, right?"

"As I see it, I had left adolescence very quickly, coming from a very strict religion in which I had believed in virginity."

"Were you a virgin?"

"Yes. I never drank alcohol but all of a sudden I let loose and went crazy, it was a year…of that."

"Sex, drugs, and rock and roll?"

"Yeah."

"Well, the next time you were with another woman, how was it? Natural?"

"I took it as it came."

"I'm not asking how you met and dated girls, but how was your next sexual encounter with a woman?"

"Yeah, well, I don't know." (She was unable to explain this encounter, but I remembered an earlier time when she talked about her sexuality after she realized she was gay and she had said, "Well, if I remember correctly, the first woman took on quite an active role.") "Well, the other person did everything."

"Even if she did everything, and you played the passive role, was there much inhibition on your part or were you all in?"

"No, no! All in!"

"Real enjoyment?"

"Yes, yes, completely wrapped up. I was certain that I wanted it and I enjoyed it very much."

"It was interesting and it was very fun. I was going through a major change, a shift in my personality. I went from being a timid person to an extrovert. I can see a real difference between my heterosexual life and my bisexual life."

"You do not identify as homosexual or lesbian?"

"No, because when there is no cake, there is still bread."[1]

Sometimes the impossibility to name oneself is part of the impossibility to accept oneself completely.

For many women it becomes natural to hide their choice[2] of sexuality. For many others it is simply not necessary to announce it. That is why we say that coming out is not a one-time thing. Instead, there are various spaces in which we have to talk about our choice and keep coming out.

In general the first time that one tells her story it is in the most intimate circle of friends. In case she has the good fortune of having siblings who are close, she may tell them.

How do you choose who to tell and who not to tell? This is a question very particular to each person. There is not just one way to do it. And many times it has to do with the desire to share what is happening with us, to share that we are in love, which is of course something to shout from the rooftops.

Also some women feel that the easiest way to say it is in response to

---

1 "No, es que cuando a veces no hay tortas, bueno es el pan." This reference to torta (cake) is a colloquial term for lesbian. The bread is referring to men.

2 Spanish "elección," meaning "choice," is understood to mean the choice to live one's sexuality. Throughout the book the question of being born gay or choosing to be gay is discussed.

someone who asks a challenging question, "Hey, you're not *tortita* are you?" But of course very few people near us would have the courage to ask that.

I've always wondered to myself why we say come out of the closet. Are we trapped living an unpleasant double life of feeling pain, condemned in a state of non-existence, of not being?

In the first moments of my discovery that I was a lesbian or homosexual, I lived with a male gay friend who always told the same joke. "When I was a kid I wanted to be a hair stylist but my mom said, no, because all male hair stylists are whores. Now I am neither a whore nor a hairstylist. Want me to comb your hair?"

What are we? How are we? What behaviors define our being or our choice? In what ways are we defined by the discourse and the words of others, or by what they think of us?

In relation to female homosexuality, that is to say, lesbians, we are generally assumed to have certain behaviors, behaviors that are products of the social imagination that, in many ways, does not adequately describe the reality of how we live and feel. One of the greatest myths is that in bed one of the women develops the role of man or macho and is confined to only that. If it is true that there is someone who takes the more active role, this role continuously changes. It is not normally decided beforehand nor is it fixed (except in some cases) and this depends greatly on each couple.

Also it is thought that the sexual experience between two women is limited to foreplay or else linked to a sexual experience with a third person assumed to be a man. Such assumptions are almost always false.

CHAPTER THREE
A Matter of Identity

The singer, Rita Lee, plays in the background in an effort to establish a good ambiance for conversation. There are questions about the book, a desire to be involved, to know what I am trying to do, what my objectives are for this project. What I bring to the talk is my belief in the necessity to communicate and the story of what I have overcome. I have moved past some of my own prejudices to be able to take better control of my life. I want to say that I have set my journey in motion and that I am able to move forward. I tell the woman I am about to interview that this is the moment to get the ball rolling.

In this moment in my life, I have the complete conviction to be and accept who I am. And from now on, I am not only a lesbian, but a *lesbian writing about lesbians.* Each daily role that we take defines us and completes us. Therefore, we are a combination of roles that we continue developing and assuming daily and each is intrinsically connected to the other. One role by itself does not define us completely. In other words, each one needs the other in order to complete us.

I could not have proposed this work of compiling stories, contacting lesbian and bisexual women, without first having gone through my own coming out of the closet. But I must clarify that this coming out of the closet, as I said before, is not a one-time thing that you do once and it lasts forever; we will face coming out again and again every day. And sometimes we will be challenged to come out and say, "Yes, you are right. I am what you say." At first it will be in a timid way, with a little flush in the cheeks, as if distilling the words little-by-little to become accustomed to the sensations. In this sense coming out can be almost like a purging, a way of understanding our own body, ridding it of thousands of toxins that pain us. But eventually, as we name ourselves, our bodies get used to the sensations of being stared at by others, of interacting with others in this new reality where we live and accept who we are.

The woman I have in front of me at the moment is named Gabriela and she explains a theory that she has. She calls it the Asterisk theory, and this theory is about what signs we look for in a woman to help us determine if she may be gay. She believes that the more characteristics a woman has that hint she may be gay, the greater likelihood the woman will develop and sustain a homosexual preference. The theory suggests that the characteristics of a gay woman exist in a latent state and can either be developed or not. If she has one characteristic such as short hair, short fingernails, plays lots of sports, has a kayak, a Jeep[1], and a cocker spaniel, she may not be gay, but the addition of more characteristics (or what this woman calls "asterisks") brings one closer to the possibility of having a homosexual experience.

These signs are not always true. Women, straight or gay, may express themselves in various manners while also being attracted to same or different sexes. Still, some lesbian and bisexual women do look for these characteristics in another woman in order to gather the courage to approach another woman.

"When did you realize that you liked women?"

"In 1998 or 1999 I was with a girl for the first time and ever since then I realized just how much of the time and for how long I had liked women. All the memories of past situations came back to me. I remember from sixth grade, when I fell for my teacher. There had been other situations that made me very happy, but I did not associate it with being a lesbian. Also, before my first time with a woman I fantasized a bit. I was around eleven years old. I was content as I began to realize this about myself, so I started to have ideas of moving to Spain."

"Spain?"

"Yes, because I thought that it was a free land! And I was not wrong because the Spanish people are pioneers in gay marriage. I needed a vacation to be in some way a little bit more myself."

---

1 Auto uno

I asked her: "You wanted to free yourself, to not have anything holding you back in saying or expressing yourself to live your fantasies?"

"Yes, to have encounters with women."

It is a common denominator in the lives of women that I have interviewed, this idea of going to a different place, "to a place that I most wished for"[2] says the song, whose author I do not remember. A place where I can live what I feel, to allow myself to be a woman in love with another woman:

To dive between words of cotton,
Smooth buds, flashes of light
And rough rivers,
Sail boats that cross the bay
Birds that shed feathers of ash
She wears birds on her head
Plovers
She has ideas that do not match with her town,
They want to make her believe
That she is wrong, but really
She believes that she has lived wrong.
One morning she left from her box,
Took off the hanging rags that had covered her body,
She left them with nothing more, at the door of the street where nothing is left,
Because she had always heard it said:
One must not leave washcloths out in the sun.
But this morning it did not matter,
She completely forgot everything,
Remembering almost nothing…
Now, it is like looking in a mirror.

---

2 A un lugar que yo más quiera.

"And how was that moment when you became conscious that you liked women?"

"I began to be attracted to a woman. In fact, I lived a fantasy. Well, also it had a lot to do with what we had discussed of characteristics and the Asterisk theory, thinking that this woman could be homosexual. It was not like the teacher I had a crush on whose romantic relationship with me was never going to happen for many reasons, one of which was the fact she was heterosexual. This time I realized that this woman also liked me, so it was different and I was able to fulfill my fantasies."

"Was it hard to accept and be conscious of this?"

"No."

"It was not at all difficult?"

"One single time, at the beginning, I had already kissed her. I said that I was not going to be able to do it all. I only said it once, but after that everything was smooth. I never felt bad with what I was experiencing. I never felt guilt. Of course in that first moment I had the feeling that I was unsure. I had to confront and break a ton of taboos, a ton of desires.

"I like this a lot", I said to myself. How can I deny this? I think we all ask ourselves that.

"Yes, yes, that happened to me, to be thinking of situations and recognize what I had experienced. But I never felt bad."

"Did you share what you were going through with someone after that? Did you wait? What did you do?"

"No, actually, different things started happening. First, I told my best friend, but it took me a year to tell her."

"And during that year, what happened? How did you live?"

"What happened was super crazy because in that story there also had been two guys who met each other at the same time that I met this girl, and we were all sort of friends. They also discovered their sexuality at the same time, so we formed a group to understand what was happening all together, which at first we did not understand very well and then we began to understand a little bit at a time."

"How old were you at that time?"

"I was already grown. Maybe because of that I did not need to tell anyone immediately. Also, everyone around me was completely heterosexual so there were not a lot of people with whom I felt safe confiding.

I had a gay friend, but that was when I was much younger. He had a difficult time coming out."

"Therefore, you all created this support group."

"Right, that is why at first I did not need to tell anyone else, but later, yes, progressively. It was then I began to feel bad because it was like living constantly in parallel worlds. I always had a birthday, a barbecue. I no longer knew what story to make up. It was really crazy. I think that this really affects the mind and makes one feel quite bad."

"Yes, the double life."

"The double life is terrible. I think that at a certain point it is unsustainable. When I could no longer manage it, I began to come out to as many people as possible and every time I told someone it turned out well."

"How so?"

"The first person I told was my best friend, a bit abruptly. It was a Thursday and we had gone out to see a band.[3] And why do the girls go? To find the boys, or meet a specific boy. That is when I told her, in that context."

"At the show?"

"Before we went out. During the entire show, my friend spent the whole time leaning on a railing, looking into the distance. I did not understand her reaction at all. She knew the girl I was going out with. It was like I threw a bucket of cold water on her face, and after that she did not ask me anything. A month went by and she did not ask me anything. She was my best friend, so one day at another club I said, "I feel really bad because you did not ask me anything about what I confided to you." She said, "I just do not want to invade your privacy." "But we are friends; it upsets me that you did not ask me anything." She apologized and that night we talked. She was the person with whom I felt the most comfortable at the time because she was my best friend. When you are dating someone, it is difficult to express yourself to people who are not gay. Well, at least at one point that was difficult for me."

"What do you mean by, 'express yourself?'"

"Kiss your girlfriend, like any other couple."

"Like a heterosexual couple?"

"Yes, exactly. And it was so strange, because the person I was most

---

3 Una peña

connected with at the time was the only person from which I felt, not rejection, but something negative. Because really, after all the times that I came out to people, which has been about a thousand times, they were all good experiences. I needed for her to have asked me more; to have asked, "How are you doing?"

The construction of our identity is a process that we have to break open, rip through the stereotypes, which many times contain our own internalized judgments. One of the most notable stereotypes is to think that we must be masculine to attract other women but it is not always like that. The same woman I was talking with said to me at one point: "I am now more feminine than ever in all my life. My appearance at this moment is the most feminine." And I believe her, because I remember seeing her in college classes and I remember asking myself, "Is that girl gay?" Strangely enough in that moment I also had not defined myself. I defined myself many years later. As one of the girls in the first interview said, "You did not have your (gay) radar on." This about the radar is really crazy; when you define yourself you begin to smell homosexuals. Could it be that a gland is activated, which vibrates and detects them? And even more curious is that you always can detect those who are not out completely, those who for whatever reason cannot openly live it and this ruins their lives. These are the ones who have a way about them and do everything in their power to hide their sexuality. It is marked on their skin and body that they are homosexual, yet they have no idea what to do about it. Their bodies speak of everything that their mouths can neither pronounce nor communicate; but the language of the body communicates continuously.

"And what did you feel when you told someone you were gay for the first time, a sensation of relief?"

"Yes, relief…yes, I do not know how to explain it, but I associate it greatly with beginning to combine parts of something that turned out to be myself! It is an important integration, because it is a question of identity. Even though I do not call myself lesbian, honestly, because I associate it with a feminist question and with many things with which I do not agree."

"What do you call yourself?"

"I am a woman who likes women, who loves women, who lives with women. I would not put a name on it. Partly yes, I am in the category that would include lesbians. It is as if I am beginning to see a more integral subjectivity. For me it was easy to come out. To share! To begin to share other daily things. I cannot imagine returning to the double life hiding who I am, that part stays far behind in the past and I do not think I could ever do it again. The effort—I had put a lot of effort, really, a lot of energy expended so that no one would notice, so that no one would associate me with the word, 'lesbian' and a woman who prefers a same sex relationship."

Gabriela said it honestly. "So that no one will notice that I am still struggling to name myself." That is the sensation we feel before we put the word "lesbian" in our mouth, but as I said earlier, our bodies communicate regardless of this silence.

When we can do this difficult task, when we can say "lesbian" or express that we love women, it feels liberating and we feel power and pride: it is a pride that many times shocks, hurts, or interrupts, as the interviewee said before. It is a pride for something we cannot describe, exactly, "pride for what and why," or maybe it is a pride of being, of living life without masks. But maybe it is also a pride in denaturing that which is so naturalized, which is to think of a woman in a romantic relationship with a man, and vice versa. There is a pride in creating a different theme, opening up the game to another possibility, to cozy up with the word 'lesbian'. When we do this we discover an unknown land of sensations and sometimes discover an abyss that opens beneath our feet. This sensation of emptiness encourages us to accept that we are at the border, breaking parameters. Finally, we allow ourselves to be seduced by a woman and to understand the beauty of it and to be excited by the experience. It is the simple fact of desire calling to us, telling us how we want it. It is no longer forbidden to us.

"And your family knows about you?"

"Yes, they do."

"All of them?"

"No, not all. With my family, it took me a while."

"And who did you tell first?"

"My mom."

"And how was the conversation? Do you remember?"

"Well, it was similar to that with my best friend. When I told my mom I was very nervous and it was crazy because I had not gone there to tell her. I went for something else."

"So what made you want to tell her? How did you decide?"

"With my family, I had been living a parallel experience, the double life. I could not tell them everything about my life even though I cared about my family and my connection to them."

"Were you in therapy?"

"I was in therapy and that accelerated the growth process greatly. And one day I went to my mom's house and she said that I never tell her anything. 'Well, you want to know something, you want me to tell you?' 'Why do I never know anything about my children?' she complained. 'You want to know, I'll tell you!'"

"And how did you tell her?"

"I remember that I got very nervous. I was beginning to mumble something and my mom said, 'Don't stress yourself, I already know!' And I was, wow! Very taken aback by her words."

"No! How did she know?"

"My mom had this 'look'—it was totally unexpected. It began like that and then I said, 'That's it; we won't discuss this again.' She gave me that look. I was not feeling well at that moment either. So, I told her, 'My girlfriend is Carolina.' And she said, 'I already know.' My brother had insinuated to her it at one point, jokingly."

"Always the brothers!!!"

"Yeah, brothers and their humor, I tell you, that is a theme for another book. And so my mom had continued thinking and I think that parents always know you, and when they don't it is because there is something that keeps them from knowing you. Also, it had been many years since I had shown any signs of being interested in men."

"Did you have many indicators?"

"Of course, all of the stereotypical attributes. I lived with a female friend, went to dinner with a female friend, always my female friends, and never had I returned to speak of a man. And when my mom once had suggested a man to me, I said, "Look mom, he is gay." I had been giving a lot of signs, and well, we ended up talking about a lot of things and we ended up relaxing so much that she said, "Hey, your cousin so and so has asterisks too, yeah?" I don't know mama; I would have to think about it. Well, she ended up sharing a lot of things about the family: "And do you remember Pato? Why Pato…. she is gay!!!!" And since then we have gotten along very well.

"There is a large percentage of women who come out as lesbian after the death of their father. Why is that? I do not know. It does not always follow the same pattern of conduct. In some cases it is because when someone so familiar and close to us dies, we feel confronted by death and we question our own manner of living life. Then the inevitable question arises; is it worth it to not allow myself to live my sexuality? Who gets hurt if I do? Who does it help if I keep quiet?

In my case it was just how things turned out when I decided to give free reign to the sexual impulses that women brought out in me and I got rid of all the prejudices and entered the exquisite territory of making love to a woman. I had only a moment to think, to consolidate this act, and then a few months passed and soon after my father died. I did not have the opportunity to tell him, but I would have loved to have been able to share it with him. And I regret having kept from him an important part of myself. Maybe we would have had a beer that day and talked for a good while. I did not have a good relationship with him, but sometimes when we were in sync we could talk for hours and hours or go on road trips.

I must say that I am the daughter of the second marriage of my mother and therefore I have brothers who are much older than I am. Many times I felt that they played the role of father for me. At that time I was not able to confront my brothers and tell them about my sexual orientation. Now that some eight years have passed since my decision I can talk about it with one of my brothers. I ask myself why I did not talk to them earlier about what was happening. At first I had told myself that it did not matter what they said or what their opinion was about the topic because really I did not have a very fluid relationship with them. But in reality talking to them would have been to confront the established order of things. My oldest brother also died three years ago, before I had the chance to share the story of my identity with him. A little while ago, in October, I wrote a letter to my brother, Luis, and I told him a little bit about my decision to live my sexuality. This year we talked about it in person and he knows that I am writing this book. He told me that my godson said, "The ones I don't like are the gay men, but I cannot say that in front of your sister." I appreciate that he does not say that to my face. "I imagine," says Luis, "that you will talk and tell about the discrimination that you all suffer." Sometimes I think that this discrimination is a ghost that is born and grows larger whenever we do not speak up or when we hide our choice of sexual affection.

The conversation develops in a fluid manner, so much so that I lose myself a little in the questions, which means I have to use my notes to see where we are going:

"Do you want to add anything?"

"About my siblings. They do not know. They know and they don't know, actually. I assume that they already guessed it because for ten years there has been no boyfriend, no anyone. I don't know what they think, that I am a plant? They no longer want to introduce me to any of their friends."

"Well, you got past that stage. You no longer rely on them for their approval and have chosen to live your own life."

"What word would you use to define yourself? Meaning, which word would you use that names your sexual orientation?"

"I define myself as a woman. I am a woman. I will not put 'lesbian' in front of that." She thinks for a moment then adds, "No, really, I would not."

"Do you like that word?"

"Lesbian? No, I associate it with a political position, an orthodox feminism that I do not agree with on many points. I believe there are things that go deeper than gender. It seems that some groups are guilty of holding prejudices internally and externally, the same things that they are supposedly fighting against. I do not feel like I can identify; I disagree, so I do not like the word 'lesbian'."

"And *tortillera*?"

"*Tortillera* is a little more derogatory than the heterosexual word for "gay." *Tortita, tortona* and *torta* are more internal to the groups. I am not sure how others would see that."

"Someone told me '*tortita*' is nicer, like 'chubby,' they said, and I like cake[4]. I'm greedy and I like cake. There are people who do not like cake; *tortita* is sweeter. And one cannot say 'pie,'[5] which has another connotation."

"I will tell you that this about words. Right now it is in vogue that

---

4 "Y me gustan las tortas" – torta is cake.
5 pastel

people use the terminology. It's good in one way but sometimes it is used in excess. How '*Tortillera*' is received depends on who, how and when it is used."

"With the intention it is used."

"With '*tortita*' also, because with '*tortita*' one can aim to say a number of things, same as lesbian. That is why for me it goes much further than the words."

"I feel the same way. '*Tortillera*' is very strong. I do not like it."

"It sounds bad, true. What I like best is '*tortita.*' I wrote it a lot as a joke."

"You would say then that the most aggravating word for you is '*tortillera?*' Or is there a different one for you?"

"No, not *tortillera*, but yes, you want to know which one is most aggravating for me? In my youth there was *marimacho* and *machona*. It seems that these all are very derogatory, but now, for a number of years I have not heard them. But when I was younger I did and I did not like it."

"Did people say it to you or to someone else?"

"No, they did not say it directly to me."

"Did you play sports? Which one?"

"Yes, volleyball, yeah. I was very sporty. The *tortita* that works out, and is very good and rigorous with sports, is a stereotype. I also think that it comes from *marimacho* = *machona* = macho = man. Very stereotypical—the lesbian must be masculine. A straight woman could have masculine characteristics and wear heels, and therefore still comply with the feminine stereotypes. I think that masculinity and femininity are deeper than who you sleep with.

"Why do you think you are lesbian? Why do you think you like women? Did you ever wonder?"

"What a good question! There are some theories."

"Is one born lesbian or does she choose it?"

"Born lesbian? No, I do not believe in nature. Everything is a cultural construction. Everything that you see is affected by a culture, based on when we are born. We are not born lesbian. And do we become lesbian? You have to think about what it means to become. I think that the stories are in the culture. They are individual and particular and I can only know what happened to me; I cannot generalize. You can put stories together. But I feel that at some point in life I met someone, this meeting could have been with a man, but it was with a woman. I cannot tell you that, 'I would never be with a guy.' That is why I tell you, 'I met a person, she was a woman, and I chose her,' but these are things that one must take apart. It is not all a choice. I never wondered about it much either."

"You never had the need to ask yourself, because you also did not have a rejection, any questioning of your sexuality."

"No, but my mom did ask me, but not like that. She asked me like parents do, 'What did I do wrong? Why is my little girl a *tortita*? Where did I mess up?'"

"Did she ask this directly to you?"

"Yes, in a conversation we had. She said to me, 'Is it something that I did wrong?' I said to her, 'Look Mom, you and dad protected me from all the shit in this world, all of it, you did not even leave anything for me to worry about. There is something that you obviously did right! Because without that I would not be able to enjoy life in general, the things that I like, to fall in love with a woman. You did something right, because if not, all of this would have been unbearable. It would have been something ugly and I would have lived it poorly. In my family, lots of things are said, but I never heard it once said, 'We must kill all the gays.' You should feel good because I am happy; I am content with my life not only with this part. I still have a long way to go, but I feel close to my desire and this also is part of what they did. That is why I do not ask often, why am I a lesbian? But I do know that it had a lot to do with crossing paths with that woman whom I met and with whom I shared much of the familiar stories, and I think that was one thing, but it could have been a man. Guys come at number fifty on my list of priorities, if I make it that far. If my girlfriend heard me say that she would kill me! More and more I realize that what I look for in relationships are more profound meetings that move me, and I believe that this does not have gender."

"Do you think it is more difficult to maintain a relationship with someone of the same sex? Does the fact you have not had relationships with men make this question more difficult to answer? Also, do you think women are as complicated as some men say?"

"The woman is an enigma, said Freud, and I do not think he was wrong. And when you are with another woman you find two enigmas. Hold on Catalina!!!"

"All very enigmatic!"

"And yes! Consider that women are biologically an enigma. I think it is more difficult for homosexual couples, both for two men and for two women, than for heterosexual couples. But in this context, I think that the real importance is the individual. There could be two women who have an extremely complicated relationship or also a guy and girl who have an extremely complicated relationship. I do not relate it to gender, it's just different."

"You do not relate relationship difficulties to a question of gender?"

"Right, the difficulties that are faced are different for a variety of reasons. One aspect is social because mainstream institutions and organizations have not traditionally supported same sex relationships (churches, government, schools, etc.). These groups have not historically offered same sex couples protection and have contributed to my feelings of isolation and anonymity. An anonymity which in many cases is terrible, yes. That is what I meant when I said in certain respects it is more difficult for gay couples than it is for heterosexual couples. For example, today I would like to go to Cairo and kiss my girlfriend on the lips. I know that ninety-nine percent of the people would turn around and not approve, like the girls of Allison that were thrown out of the bar[6]. Prejudice is not right. Same sex relationships are more susceptible to discrimination and lack legal protection in many countries. Also, the fact that you have two women makes the situation unique. Not necessarily more difficult but, yes, unique.

When women get involved, interwoven with each other in a relationship, they can experience very intense emotions and connections. Sometimes this makes for a wonderful attraction but this same attraction can also be the very thing that drives them apart."

---

6 This refers to a bar in Rosario, Santa Fe Argentina where two girls were thrown out in 2006 for kissing while playing pool. Afterwards, many LGBT+ organizations in Rosario went to the bar and staged a kiss-in to protest the bar's mistreatment of LGBT people.

CHAPTER FOUR

Love In the Times of Chat

She started by saying my name while holding a cigarette nervously in her hand, but on her face—a beautiful smile.

Perhaps she agreed to talk with me about her life because she already knew me? Or maybe because I persuaded her with my passionate speech to participate? Or maybe because she felt something different in me?

I could not ask myself these silly questions or think about seducing her. I maintain my role to find out basic information: Nadia is at this moment the youngest woman that I have talked to in order to find out more about her lesbian experience. She is only twenty-one and has been living her sexuality for six years with absolute impudence. She herself says that she is "precocious and postmodern."

Faced with these words I cannot help but wonder: Is this what it means to be lesbian? Or perhaps homosexuality was not a habitual conduct throughout history

We can find information that tells us the majority of ancient cultures have considered lesbians to be nonexistent (with the exception of Greece). Male homosexuality, on the other hand, was considered long ago and then categorized by more modern peoples as an illness. Now same sex relationships are not classified as "sick" in medical literature—at least not in the West. Historically, women were more likely to be harassed for being adulterers and prostitutes, but not for our choice of lovers. It is in this respect that lesbians could be considered marginalized by omission and not by recognition.

I wonder if it would be sufficient to continue looking for this recognition to make our rights complete, feeling certain that the Church will never change its condemnation, whereas the rest of society has moved forward. Could it be that the Church will never change its opinion on this topic, or will it continue updating it as it did previously with the question of divorce?

Nadia lit up another cigarette. Now calmer, she smiled at me again. She was truly beautiful and with skin so fresh, so soft, anyone would desire to lie down with her and let herself go. She looked at me with uncertainty, a latent anxiety. She approached the computer and with a hand on the mouse, she continued to look at me intensely. She asked, "What would you like to listen to?" Joaquin Sabana was singing in the background, *"Peor para el sol"*... and I say, "This is good... I like it."

The meeting was in the intimacy of her apartment, which was cozy and small. She shared it with her older brother with whom at times, she explained to me, they have a habit of bringing home women at the same time, in which case they alternate bedrooms.

I went over to the window to get a little air as the cigarette smoke and the situation restricted my breathing a bit. She came up behind me, subtly grazed my body with hers, reached her hand over my shoulder and pushed back the curtain. We could see the neighbor hanging clothes out to dry on the line. Nadia looked at the neighbor and said, "She always comes up at this time. I like to watch her. She is pretty." Now there were two of us watching the neighbor in silence. She had long hair that flowed freely down her back. She wore jogging pants and slippers and her butt looked firm. She made a half turn and we discovered her face, soft skin and relaxed features.

"How old is she?" I asked.

"I don't know, about forty."

The neighbor exited the scene, interrupting our spectacle and we sat down at the table. I took out my notebook and the mp3 player. She watched me and said,

"I thought that you only took notes."

I explained that I took notes to assist my memory, especially to remember her gestures which the mp3 could not pick up. I also explained

I needed to have her words recorded. She finished her cigarette and without pause asked me a first question.

"Do you want me to tell you about the first time I had sex with a woman, or how I knew I was gay?"

I asked her to tell me how she first discovered she was gay.

"I realized I was gay without understanding really what it meant. I was in preschool. Actually, in my infancy I liked one of my friends. It turned out she was the woman I was with for the first time."

I began to feel more and more comfortable with her. Comfortable? It was something more. I began to feel attracted to her. But I was the interviewer, the one asking the questions, and I could not mix the roles or afford to be seen as unprofessional. And she, without perceiving what was happening to me, continued talking naturally.

"This continued happening with me in first and second grade, and then in high school I felt that this is how it would be, that I would like women."

"When you realized that you liked women, how did you live your life after you knew it?"

"I had to suffer with it. I did not enjoy feeling attracted to another woman and so I hid myself in clothing, wearing all black. And I even wrote in code until I was eighteen."

"In code! How was that?"

"I continued expressing what I felt in a small notebook, writing in code in case someone were to read it."

"You had created your own language, to be able to express what was happening to you?"

"Yes, only I knew how to decipher what it said. And even more, to be able to express myself I wrote backward so that no one would understand. It was difficult to go look for a notebook; I did not want to write. I resisted facing who I was; I did not want to be different because I felt that I would feel alone, disliked, with no one who would understand me. What color do you think I used to express myself?" She asked me and paused waiting for my response. "I opened my closet and everything was black, because that is the color of how I felt until the moment came when I knew that I had to take off the mask and reveal myself. Prior to that moment I thought I would prefer to be rejected or judged. I felt alone and distant from everyone during that time. After I turned eighteen, I spoke with my family and came out to them. At first, coming out to my family didn't change my sense of isolation. I still suffered a lot and felt very alone, even when I was with a close friend who knew about me."

Like Nadia, we have a necessity to name ourselves despite the difficulty of doing so. Often, somehow, we escape from the language that names us. But some of us find certain devices that permit us to name ourselves outside of the active discourse, establishing a territory of words that constitutes us as beings, as subjects.

Nevertheless, sometimes we still hide ourselves and deny who we are because at first it is so difficult to accept ourselves for who we are.

I wanted to imagine how her first loving nights in the arms of a woman had been and my mind took me back to my first night with a woman, my first kiss. I remember that mouth capturing mine, that tongue looking for mine, following along my body, making my body hers. I remember the anxiety of those first nights, the sensation of crossing the boundaries into a forbidden territory, a territory absolutely prohibited. I can still feel in my body remnants of those sensations of discovering my body together with hers as if we were one. Untiring explorers of ecstasy, we went discovering more and more new sensations, combining manners, imagining poses, trying, feeling and making love in our own language and enjoying the craziness of it.

"And how was it with the girl? You met up, had sex and did not talk?"

"We met up and we got drunk because we had made plans for later that evening. I think we both knew what would happen afterwards. We got together with a group and we could not look each other in the eye, even though there were knowing chuckles between us, embarrassment, fear that the other girls would find out. I think that these things were quite tense for both of us and we repressed ourselves a lot and hid what was happening. It was not something that I enjoyed."

"The first time that you were with your friend, did you make love with a certain embarrassment?"

"I suppose that we felt the same embarrassment that any adolescent feels their first time kissing another adolescent. I think that for heterosexuals it is the same, with the difference that, in my case, we did not speak. Even with my partner."

"Not even with others?"

"With no one. Even more, I feared that people I cared about would find out and this drove me to want to hide my identity and my new self-knowledge with all of my soul, although with my body I mostly feared that I would catch something contagious."

We laughed a lot about this last comment she made. I remember that I had a similar discomfort thinking that I would be discovered. For me it was fear of being discovered by my friends and family but also the fear of being discriminated against. I had enormous fear those I cared cared about would stop loving me if I told tell them I was a lesbian.

And so I share with you, from my current position of tranquility, that I overcame this bad feeling."

"Did you think that you were going to disappear or become a pariah to others?"

"No, not necessarily, but I worried that someone would find out and I would be abandoned. It was such a taboo topic at the time."

Nadia's story was in some ways very similar to mine and I imagine, to many other stories, full of fears and reproaches, fear of losing the tenderness and acceptance. We are taught to be a certain way, outside of which nothing is accepted or acceptable. And therefore we convert ourselves into rare specimens, nocturnal sinners, guilty of loving in a different way, beings that definitively do what we want and feel, but sometimes in hiding.

"So, after that how did you cope with telling others, confiding that you were woman who loved women? How did you come to terms with accepting yourself?" That *is* the topic, right—when we begin to put who we are into words?"

"I think that I began to accept who I was, and to fill my closet with color, to desire the sun, because I hated the sun before. I hated everything that had to do with life. When I came out to my family is when I first began to accept myself because I said, 'This is who I am and I carry it forward and take control of it. I want this life and I do not want to repress myself anymore, or write in code, or wear black. I do not want to listen to bad, strong, violent music.' I began to change. From then on I began to accept myself. I knew that I was going to be this way, but I still could not talk about it to anyone. I was uneasy about other people finding out."

"And when was the first time you told someone? When you said, 'I am this' how did you express it to your family, to your mom? Were they all there?"

"There were two distinct coming out moments that I remember. First, I came out to my family and second, to my friends. I will tell you about my family and after that about my friends. It was a Saturday and I was at my house. The phone rang and it was Veronica, one of my friends. My mom was getting ready to go to a party. She was in that festive mood, the one in which all is well and in which you think that nothing can ruin the party. Veronica had a masculine voice and behavior and my mom commented, after we hung up, that people said that Veronica was in a relationship with a girl (which was true!) and that she had been for at least four years. Then she asked, 'What is it with Veronica that she has somewhat masculine characteristics? Is she with that girl?' This was the first time that I had spoken with my mom about homosexuality. I got really nervous when we sat down to talk. My palms sweated, my heart raced fast."

"Tachycardia?"

"Something like that. At first I said, 'Look, Mom, I do not know why Veronica is the way she is.' But finally I found the courage and said, 'Yes!' I shouted. 'What do you mean 'yes?'' Mom said. 'Yes!' (I did not know what else to say). 'Yes she is happy with Mara. What? Is that bad?!' 'No, no,' Mom said, 'I did not say that it was bad.' I wanted to see how she reacted. I wanted to evaluate how my mom would take the news about Veronica in a kind of test to see what would happen if I told her the same thing happened with me. At that time I was with a girl who was from my town and who had been accepted into our group. I had met her through a friend and it became something important, a relationship of six months I think, so my mom asked me about it. I could see that she suspected. She denies it now, but she noted something in me. I had some masculine characteristics, behaved differently from the norm, and was told that I was odd. My sister Virginia was totally different from me. When my mom asked me about Veronica, I said that she was happy, blah, blah, blah. And she said to me, 'What is up with you, are you the same as she is? Why does this girl come visit you? She was not part of your group before. What happened that she is now part of your life here?' I confessed to her that, yes, I liked this girl she had mentioned, that she was my girlfriend and that I loved it! I told her even more, that I wanted to be with her and that I had been with a woman before. I told her everything."

"You spilled it all."

"Everything! We hugged, she cried and said, 'I suffer, not because of this inclination that you have, but rather I cry for everything that you have suffered in this time that you have not talked to anyone. How did you not tell us sooner?' Later she told my father. She went to the party that night—with this new information. The next day we got up and she said, "We are going to Rosario to talk to your siblings." I actually was concerned with how the rest of my family would react. At first I could not look anyone in the face and even more I felt fear of my brother. I feared that he would think that I looked at his girlfriends, even though sometimes I did," she confessed jokingly. "I did not know how he would take it, so I did not look around much because I did not want this to be happening to me. I was in the famous stage which my friend and I call the 'why me?' stage because I did not want this to happen to me."

"How did you respond to this stage?"

"It is a question that I asked myself at the time but I did not have an answer. Why me? What is happening to me? Why am I like this? Why is it not happening to others?"

In the beginning we deny these different sensations, the things that happen to us that we cannot manage, and so we mistreat ourselves. We deny ourselves, we escape. I remember that for much of the time in my adolescence, even if I did not recognize that I repressed my gay senti-ments. I needed to hit the pavement and run like an outlaw, eight or ten kilometers each day, with a desire to escape feeling who and what I was. I wanted to distance myself greatly from something that I could neither name nor imagine. During this time I was about fifteen years old. I felt attracted to my neighbor's cousins. At the time I thought that it was only a question of admiration and a necessity to identify myself with them. Now I know that it was pure attraction, an attraction that burned and overwhelmed me."

"With what word do you define yourself?"

"As a *torta*, super lesbian. I define myself like that, both gay and postmodern in my dialect."

"Do you think that for women it is more difficult to accept and live our gay lives than for gay men?"

"To me that is relative. It depends on the person. I think it is difficult in both cases. What happens is that some think there are fewer gay women than gay men. But whether that is true or not, it does not have much impact on my experience as a lesbian woman."

As our conversation progressed, I continued to welcome and enjoy the sound of her voice. I felt as if her voice would cover me in laughter, exuding warmth as we shared in complicit glances, talked of shared parties, of salt and honey, of laughter and skin. I felt a supreme happiness when she said such things as, "We are inundated." Yes, flood me with your waters and waves. With great strength I settled myself and asked:

"And what is the word that defines your sexual condition and to which word would you say, 'I do not like that word.'?"

"The one that I reject?"

"Yes."

"The typical: *tortillera*. I accept and use *torta*. But I am likely to speak up and open the mind of someone who calls me *tortillera*. I do not know if it just hits me wrong or if it lashes out at me. Do not think that I am going to go to my house and cry, unable to leave because someone called me a *tortillera*. I do not shut myself in anymore."

"Do you think it is difficult to maintain a loving, affectionate relationship?"

"Relationships that last a long time are rare. Today, generally the relationships of a couple do not last long, and even more so in our circle. It has become normal now that everyone is part of a group that is connected to another online and they chat with whomever. That is how we go forming touch-and-go relationships and this wears on any relationship. What undermines human relationships is not the internet but the messages where there is much hysteria. 'Today I talked with her, I chatted with another.' This undermines and tends to devalue couples' relationships. This also happens to me. I am part of this, immersed in it."

"Do you mean that you note a virtualization of human relationships?"

"Yes, I note that there is little transparency in the people with whom we relate. We often doubt and question the authenticity of the people we are supposedly 'in relationship' with because of the cell phone, the internet, or because of the places we frequent. There are those we sometimes meet with whom we have little or nothing in common, yet all these things happen—sleeping around, superficial relationships, etc. So I think that partly this is the reason relationships do not last. There is a lot of history and there is a massive amount of information.

We arrived at the end of Nadia's story with night approaching, and we kissed. The mp3 player finally turned off, we kept talking for a long time more while enjoying the effects of the margaritas.

CHAPTER FIVE

A Coming Out Story Told in a Bubbly and Refreshing Manner

In my personal life there was a moment where I confirmed how good freedom feels and how it brings one to full happiness. I really was not conscious or open to the possibility of being lesbian. But then at twenty-three years old, having just ended a long-term relationship with a man a few months before, it was a special moment in my life. Partly because I had met two new gay male friends (who had only recently begun their relationship) I began to let my curiosity flow.

My friends remember me saying: "Look I believe in love. I don't know in what form it will come, though," as I shared my feelings between their smiles and snickers. Now I tell myself, "How wonderful to know that I am looking for love in the right type of person!" You probably already know about the informal methods of investigation and research. They are the usual ones: online chat rooms, gay websites, gay bars, coffee houses and restaurants, etc. It turned out that my new gay friends began to pressure me to define myself. They even labeled me, 'the undefined'. I heard it all the time until I went out one night, a gay bar in town, to see how I felt. "Ok," I said, "so now you guys can't call me 'the undefined' anymore. Stop messing with me about it."

I left the bar with a smile on my face! My heart was leaping from my chest. There I discovered that I adored the gay scene; I felt a special energy, something like wanting to release myself to a more sexy and sensual world. And so it came; I had my first lesbian relationship to feel it. I think that in that week I created in my mind thousands of sexual experiences with women. I knew how soft it would be, how sensual I would feel, and that is something I loved a lot. Friends, *stop calling me undefined.* I like women *a lot, a lot,* and *this is where I am staying.*

I was beginning to know myself at last. I looked to surround myself with people I could share the good news with while I continued to study and do my own research. Of course, soon after I first discovered and accepted I loved women, I decided I wanted a stable partner. I only needed to find someone else who desired that too. You know what? Now I see the memory of this time as one of the two things in my life that has enabled me to feel strong and to be myself.

During one's entire life there will be continuous situations of coming out of the closet to friends, work, and family. In each situation you reaffirm and you continue to grow. But that one face, that sensation that I felt when I left the bar that first night, wow! I needed to—and I always will—remember that.

CHAPTER SIX
One Must Break In Order to Build

When we work with technology, we have a habit of losing information through silly and involuntary mistakes. That is what happened to the conversation and recording with this woman, and luckily I was able to record it again.

When I interviewed her for the first time, an important first meeting of lesbian and bisexual women in the city of Rosario had just taken place. I had only known her through photos and from reading comments about her activism and subsequent visibility. I knew that she had two children. I must confess that when I went to her house and saw them swarming all around, it made me a bit uncomfortable. She certainly saw it reflected on my face because immediately she calmed me by saying, "Don't worry, the kids know." The second interview I did a few months later was the same—in her house with the kids running around, with Cata, her daughter, jumping and playing with her dog near us, and Facu, her son, in his room upstairs singing out loud, "*Celebra la vida.*[1]" And I think that it is his mother who gives him a clear example or invitation to practice what the words of that song say.

"How and when did you realize that you liked women?"

"There are two possible answers: One is when I was able to live it and the other is, that I knew since I was very young. I was only able to live it in my adulthood at a more mature age, but before being able to

1 Celebrate life.

do this I wanted to achieve a few important goals and what I felt were mandates for my life. There was not one that I did not complete. In other words, I had to finish my studies, become a social worker (how shocking!) a role of assistance and caring for others. I also took on the demand of maternity. I married a man as was expected and only after all of this, all of it, could I say, 'The moment has come for me to decide, to choose what I want.'"

"Was there a moment when you chose to be conscious of your attraction?"

"More than conscious, I would say, for me, the death of my father was significant in my confronting my inner truth. You see how the idea of death generates some consciousness of life, and so it was very impactful for me. My dad had been sick since he was thirty, and he lived until fifty-four years old with two possible choices: One was to have an operation with a fifteen percent chance of being cured and the rest of that percentage to die. The other option was to accept his disability and not be able to work anymore. He chose to have the operation against the wishes of the family, and beyond that, my mother felt that he had abandoned her. To me his position was very dignified and this is what allowed me to make the decision to take charge of what was happening to me and what had been happening to me but that I had not given space."

"Was it immediately after the death of your father or some time after?

"I would say that things continued to happen—me getting in touch with my feelings, first falling in love with a professor, the relationship which was impossible. She later became my director, which was a place of great authority. She was much older than I was and she was not ever going to give the relationship any serious consideration. She was inaccessible. I had to fall in love from an idealized and unreal place."

"Did this happen before the death of your father?"

"It was before, but I was not conscious that it was love, I saw it as fantasy, as something that had no explanation."

"You could not give it a name."

"Of course I could not. I started therapy (I did four years of therapy while I was with the father of my children)."

"Did you start therapy because of what was going on internally with your attraction to women or for something else?"

"I started therapy for something else, but my attraction to women was the latent reason. And whenever we discussed the topic, the psychologist said that they were fantasies until my father died and I went off on a trip and met a woman. Nothing happened with *us*, but for *me* a lot happened. And that made me decide to separate from my husband."

"So you can say that at that time you became conscious of the possibility to choose a woman as a partner to love?"

"Yes, totally, from that moment on it was as if I could not directly control the situation."

"It was as if I had given myself permission to desire. The unconscious was stronger than the level of repression my consciousness was engaged in. And this meant that I had to take another type of action, an action to give myself liberty to what was happening to me. That is why I gave two possible answers to the question you asked about when I first knew I was attracted to women. One is always, because the sensation was always there. What happened is that it was so repressed due to the expectations we are taught. That is why, because of others, we do not see what we are feeling. We do not understand it or permit ourselves to feel."

"Of course one does not see it as a possibility for one woman to choose to love another woman to create a family, a couple."

"It is not part of what we learn and therefore, since it is not part of what we are taught it is difficult to realize what is happening to us, to give words to what never had words."

"How was the moment when you met the woman and thought about it and things happened inside you? How did you feel about your life after that?"

"It was not easy—an internal revolution, pain and at the same time I was experiencing these feelings without having any past history with a woman—not any woman for a long time until I resolved my current situation at the time which was more than anything about the relationship with my husband. But I had the sensation of a constant internal struggle, which was not easy. It generated much tension. I have always said that in order to do, one must undo. And in this undoing one must do things that cause pain, explain to my children, explain this to my family, to my mother. All of these things meant that yes, before being a lesbian from a point of practice, I was a lesbian politically. What does that mean? First, I felt lesbian, I recognized myself, I called myself lesbian and since I named myself I could not see any other way to live except activism. This had a lot to do with my personal history, that since I was sixteen years old I have fought. This is the way I have chosen to live, that if I am a lesbian I will continue to be an activist."

"You cannot separate activism from being lesbian?"

"It is very difficult for me to accept life, society, the system as it is. Really, I am always thinking of transforming it. And the same happened to me with my sexuality; it was very difficult for me to accept myself. At first, I was thinking that I would be able to improve the conditions of life for people who make a choice of sexual affection that is different from the rest. And from that point on I began to fight. Before having an experience with a woman I went to a group for lesbians and to meet women."

"You could say that you made the journey uniquely yours and different from other women."

"For sure, I went to the meeting of lesbians. Even more, the first time I went I said that I did not have orgasms. That was all that I could think of to say. I was shaking because I did not know what to say and the feminist lesbians attacked me because there are plenty of heterosexual women who do not have orgasms and that fact by itself does not make them homosexuals. But of course my saying that was not to suggest that it had, specifically, anything to do with my desire and difficulty to name myself."

"There is an expectation that says that the woman must have an orgasm. What they did not tell me was how to have an orgasm, or that some women climax one way and others another way. Or that penetration was not necessary in order to have an orgasm. Or that some women need stimulation of the clitoris in order to climax—many different things. For example, I had not even heard anyone talk about the clitoris. I knew that, yes, I needed to have an orgasm, but I was never told how to. Or I was told of just one way that I had to achieve one.

"Of course I was also told the only proper way was the heteronormativity of intercourse and that the only legitimate relations were ones that focused on phallic and genital-centric activity to the exclusion of any other type of eroticism. In my case the heteronormative model was certainly not what motivated me, what moved me."

"Once you said, 'Well, I am a lesbian,' once you named yourself, who was the first person you told?"

"The woman I had something with for the first time…Ha, had

something, I did not have anything. Five hundred thousand things happened to me, but at least I was able to talk to her about my feelings."

"And what did you tell her?"

"That I liked her and well...nothing. That I did not know what to do with what was happening to me. I began to talk about my children and how difficult it was to accept my feelings. What gave me the most fear was that my choice might cause pain to my children."

"Do you think that you brought pain to your children with this choice?"

"No more than any father or mother does when they are faced with difficult choices that affect their children. Children are not spared from life conflicts. This was the conflict that I had connected to my identity and for them it was not easy at first to accept my different sexual definition. But it also depends a lot on the personality of each child; they each took it differently. But nonetheless, it was not too complicated. Each accepted the change from completely distinct places. Catalina, for example, told me, 'Yes, Mama, I know, I already know that you like women.'"

"She told you this before you even told her anything?"

"Yes, I told her that I wanted to tell her something, and she said, 'I know, I already know that you like women.'"

"How did she know?"

"I do not know. I had been processing it and she had been watching me. At the time I told her, Catalina and I already had a close relationship. And with Facundo, my son—when I told him he said, 'I don't like it' and he ran away to cry. I told him that maybe I did not like the freckles on his face, but he was my son and I loved him, that I could not choose this, just as much as he could not choose to not have freckles, that he had them and it was a question of accepting each other. And when you love someone you love them as they are. So he hugged me and told me that there was no problem. Since the beginning I have not had any problems with the children surrounding sexual identity. I have worked on it a lot with my children. I understand that it is important that they understand why I fight but recently Facu asked me on Pride Day, 'Mama, why do you always have to be on TV? Because my friends ask me.' 'What do they ask you?' 'They tell me, I saw your mom on TV.' But what do they tell you, something bad? 'No, no.' 'But do they ask you anything about what I said?' 'No, no.' 'Then why does it bother you?' 'Because I don't want them to ask me.' Of course as he reaches adolescence he will face the complexities related to sexual definition and his own sexuality. Also, we have to consider how every adolescent must differentiate himself from his parents. We can't predict or control ahead of time how our children will navigate through these 'rites of passage.'"

"Do you worry about this time in your son's life?"

"Yes, I do. I also carry the burden that I left a stable relationship to be with a woman and broke the heterosexual norm along with the monogamous norm and the treasured norm of family stability. Then I began to have sporadic relationships, and this also created waves. Suddenly, the children looked for everything that created stability. They also had a strong bond with my husband. We had been a family and I suppose when we split this caused them a certain amount of pain."

"They almost had to take it apart in order to reconstruct something else, as you said."

"They had to reconstruct and I had to reconstruct myself. To think about myself and the kids and the possibility of new relationships I might pursue is a lot to digest. As the future unfolds I foresee challenges when it comes time for me to introduce them to people who may (or may not) fill this place of family. Though not impossible, the potential challenges seem imposing."

"Well, do you think that homosexuality is a choice or a conduct?"

"I consider that it is both of these. We come back to the same thing having heard many lesbians talk about their experiences. Many say they were born lesbian. This was not my case. I believe as a social worker that everything is a construction, nothing is given. We have genetic questions, but those are the least influential in my opinion. Everything else is social, cultural, historic, and from this mixture comes our identity. So I consider that homosexuality or lesbian identity is also a construction, an identity that comes along with human growth and development. That is why I can say that my first definition of lesbian is not the same way I define the word today. Today I live it in another way and I could say the same for many other aspects of life and identity. It is like any other concept in life; it continues redefining itself with life, with the experiences that we live."

"In other words, for you the definition of lesbian has been mutating with time? It is not the same to say 'lesbian' now as when you first defined yourself?"

"Yes, yes, like everything in life. The concepts are socio-cultural and historic. To call myself lesbian is a concept also and I hope that at some point defining myself in this way will be avoidable. In other words that one day it will not be necessary to label ourselves. Today this is obligatory because there are many inequalities and no visibility and no recognition. This denies us rights, it denies us possibilities. You leave the obligatory heterosexual norm and become invisible through other realities. From this place it is necessary to name oneself in order to be seen, to become visible and to be able to demand what it is that we need. I do think that identity is a mutant construction, a changing one."

"Yes it is as changing as any process, even more so when we consider the cultural and social aspects."

How was sex with a woman for the first time?"

"How was it? Really lovely, I remember I kept saying, 'Oh, God! Oh, God!' And I remember that the other day I read your poem that talked about seeing the face of God."

She made reference to a poem that I had put on my blog which says this:

A Word

To give birth
The words
Spurting
Bidding with great strife
Blowing
The wind
Fading the time.

God
Is a word
Birthed from my mouth
In other days.

God is woman
And beautifully dressed
She wears clothes of silk and cloth,

And rouge on her lips,

Her mouth is the birthplace

Of blasphemy and orgasms

And her eyes

Come to be born rivers of tears

Which undermine

Mountains and myths,

Of presumptions

Of things said even in other languages.

She continued, "Or of the goddess. The poem speaks of the goddess. To me it felt so similar to what happened to me in that moment, it was a sensation of omni (all), a sense of totality, which I had never before been able to experience. The totality of something *is* powerful, right? Even though I did not name it at that moment. The feeling was majestic."

"What about your first sexual experience with a woman had the greatest impact on you?"

"The fact I took an active role in the situation. I surprised myself. I freed myself from the notion that I was not able to dominate, that I could not be the one to have power which broke the stereotype of women having to be more passive. Knowing I could take an active position gave me new belief in what I could do. And next I discovered my clitoris. For example, I had been getting to know my body through masturbation, but it was nothing like when you are with another person."

"And before that first time, had you imagined sex with a woman?"

"Yes, yes, in fantasies…but they did not correspond to reality. Thanks to the fantasies, however, I survived many situations, right? But even more satisfying was the knowledge that the reality is superior to the fantasy."

"Reality is better than fiction. In your case was that true?"

"Yes, totally. I remember that always with my male partner, when the interaction ended and he turned around it did not matter to him if I had an orgasm or not. On the other hand, in my first sexual interaction with a woman there was a different emotional quality to it, a different skin, a different physicality, a different dynamic. I felt freer. I was not dominated by the genital and this new freedom energized me a lot. I remember when we finished and my partner said to me, 'I do not believe that you have never been with a woman.' I felt very comfortable with what she said because my big fear was, "What if I do not know what I am doing?"' And her words were very affirming.

"Sometimes we do not know what we already know."

"After that, did you feel fulfilled?"

"Yes, totally, it was a very beautiful experience."

"With what word do you identify yourself? With lesbian, or is there another word?"

"That is the one that fits me best because to me the word lesbian is a political construction. I believe it has a lot to do with the representation of how others see us. Many times we take these representations and try to change the content to give them a new meaning but the meaning is based on how others see us. The term, 'lesbian', is a term that we construct and is, more than anything, political. That is the side where I want to position myself."

"And what word that is typically used to name women who love women offend you?"

"None of them offends me. I think that words are offensive in themselves only when they are used in such a way to wound or offend a person or group. I do not recognize an offensive word based only on the word itself. I have more fear of the motives and intentions of those using the words. Finally, what is more problematic for me than the words that are used is the potential for violence and discrimination based on gender, class, race, culture, or any other category used to exclude or diminish human beings."

"Violence sometimes is symbolic and is exercised in words."

"Yes, I agree. In fact I think that sexist language is already offensive in itself. It motivates me to change some of these linguistic rules. I am more motivated to position myself on the side of rights than from the place of victim. I feel better joining with those who want to do something to make change rather than joining with the ones who complain, 'They are offending me.' I prefer to empower myself and to be in a place where I can actively create change."

"What does visibility mean to you?"

"To be who you are, wherever you go. To be free at work, at a hospital, with your partner and show your affections, to not have to hide. Enough of the closet! We would like to have the same privileges that heterosexuals enjoy. When they ask me, 'Why do you always have to say you are a lesbian? What is the reason for that?' The importance to me is to make known that my choice is different and that because of this difference my way of relating with others will be different and my needs will be different. It is an attitude; visibility is a question of attitude toward life and this process never ends. Every day we are coming out of the closet. But each time we feel more secure in doing so and each time we are healthier for it. Being in the closet for such a long time, because of ourselves, because of the internal lesbophobia, has psychological consequences to the health of lesbians and to all of those close to us. Sometimes we believe that we do something good for others by hiding ourselves. On the contrary, we do no good for anyone or for society by remaining invisible and generating an unreality, pretending we do not exist."

I agreed with the majority of what she said. I remember when the lesbian-feminist movement first looked to establish visibility for lesbian women. Groups of women came from the most conservative sectors of society to scream into the open air. We argued many times that the only act that made homosexual women visible was to show up at lavish demonstrations of affection or tenderness and kiss in public places. As if kissing in public was the only way to gain visibility. Another theory stressed the importance of privacy and encouraged us *not* to discuss the existence of lesbians at all, lecturing that sex and everything that came with it was a private and personal matter and, therefore, should remain private and personal.

Luckily, the collective movements of LGBT groups continued to fight for rights which made it possible to be a part of the public agenda. Independent researchers like Ernesto Meccia conducted research and could say in his book *La cuestión gay*: "When it was no longer possible to stop the identity movements, the State said, 'We will stop saying what we have been saying. We have provoked a fire; we will try to put it out. It is no longer a perversion, it is no longer an illness; homosexuality is a private act and as with all human conduct we must tolerate it.' But in this, Meccia cautioned, "there is a trap, because tolerance at first is associated with the private but the private sphere does not reach to the entire expression of your personality. When a homosexual allows himself to appear gay and acts outside of the private sphere, tolerance shows its other face which is intolerance."[2]

It is common to hear people say about gay men, "I do not have a problem with homosexuals, but it bothers me when they show it." Some gay men may be more visible but not all are outwardly obvious to the public. However it does happen that some gay men show feminine characteristics just as some lesbians tend to have masculine attitudes or behaviors. These ways of being are forms of natural expression for some and for others a way to make one's sexuality visible, to show that they are making a different choice of romantic partner.

Visibility encompasses more than the idea of being able to kiss in public. It goes further than this one, everyday act which is permitted to all heterosexuals and is taken for granted by the majority. Visibility also includes rights that the heterosexual majority enjoys like the right of insurance proceeds after death, the right to share obligations in the case of a partner who has children, or if a couple decides to have or adopt children, the right to the social position of the spouse and many other rights.

Later after a long debate, with much social commentary and discussion, the decree 1054/2010 was followed by the law 26.618 which modified the Civil Code to allow marriage between people of the same sex in all of Argentina.

Finally, and with pride, we can now say these rights and obligations apply equally to the lives and families with homosexual parents, children and spouses in Argentina. Happily, those of us who desire to get married can now exercise this right and have legal and social protections we didn't have before.

---

2 *Meccia Ernesto. La cuestión gay, un enfoque sociológico. Gran Aldea Editores. 2006, Buenos Aires.*

CHAPTER SEVEN
I Do Not Like Women, My Girlfriend Is a Lesbian

The next woman who told me her story was someone I met previously when she and her girlfriend attended a party, *La Machadera*. The party took place at the school of engineering at the university we attended. This was where the first meeting of lesbians took place. I also knew of her because she was a fanatic of my blog at one time.

I only know a few details about her and next to nothing about her homosexual awakening. Partly this was due to the simple fact that it was difficult for her to accept herself. Practically speaking, she had yet to come out of the closet. Luckily, I spoke with her girlfriend, Valeria, on chat the other night and she agreed to meet with me and bring me up to date on some of the details.

Valeria and I met up in a bar and looked for a discrete place to talk, even though there was not much to choose from. The place was crowded and the patrons created a bustling and busy environment. I thought that voice recording was going to be an impossible task, so to capture her story I not only used the mp3 player but a digital microphone as well. Transcribing the recording was a difficult task because the voices on the recording were not always easy to hear.

Up until that time I had not explained much about the book to

Valeria, so before beginning our conversation, the woman asked me to tell her more.

I began to tell her about the project, the objectives I was looking for, and a little about the women whom I had interviewed for the book. She asked, "What is the most interesting story you have heard so far?"

I told her that I thought all of the stories were interesting. Each story told about a life experience and gave a glimpse of the difficulty to accept oneself as different in a world where everything is normalized. This is the same world where you are expected to act and to feel the same way that the majority feels. There is pressure to conform, as if you must copy ways of being that are foreign to yourself to remain within the majority's rules. This creates internal battles and tensions that wear you down. You feel torn between the desires of how others expect you to be and your own desires. What's at stake is the desire to be happy and look for love. Because that is what the journey is about, to be happy with a lover while knowing you are different from others."

My listener soon got hooked on the topic and began to talk about her experiences, laughing a lot. Maybe it was her way of getting rid of some of the tension in expressing herself to me. When I realized that it was important to record the things that she was saying, I interrupted her to ask if I could turn on the electronic devices to record her voice. She agreed. That is how the following story began.

She told me that with women she learned to understand her own body. So I asked,

"Understand your body?"

"I realized I could create with a woman what I was unable to create with a man. I did not realize what I could feel with another woman! Is this too confusing?"

"Not at all, that happened to me. I did not realize the pleasure that I could give and receive with a woman. I think we are much more expressive."

"Yes, that is it, exactly."

"How did you realize that you liked women?"

"I don't know! How do you realize that you see something and you like it? You like it, you like it, ha. I don't know, I liked these women in particular at that moment. I do not know if I like all women; I do not know if I would become desperate from looking at a girl's ass."

I think that there is a stigma we are thought to be promiscuous and with that we have to include gay men. But actually lesbians do not like all women, just as heterosexuals do not like every one of the opposite sex. Obviously there are contrary cases."

"How did you become conscious that you could be with a woman or choose a woman to love?"

"Basically, there was a woman who chose me and I accepted. It was a gratifying experience and, interestingly…religious."

As I said before, she laughed a lot and stretched-out words giving them a suspenseful tone. She had great control of her voice and seemed to indicate her profession in every word she said. I had to laugh at her crazy laugh. Not only was the conversation interesting, it was also funny. Wanting to maintain my composure as a professional, I did not want to lose the thread of the interview. So I continued.

"Religious, why?"

"I met her at church…(nervous laugh)."

At church we got to know each other and after services one evening, she asked me if I would like to go out for coffee."

"And why did you accept the invitation to coffee?"

"I accepted the invitation out of sexual curiosity with the idea the two of us might be able to play in a sexual way. There was a certain physical chemistry between us even though we had not talked about our feelings at that point. But I was not with anyone else at the time so it seemed fine to me. Why not? And even more, she was very pretty. You have seen the girls who hang out in groups and all get up at once. Suddenly she was in front of me asking me if I wanted to get physical and I said, 'I cannot say no to this.'"

"Where were you? How did she approach you?"

"How was it? We were in her car."

I was anxious to know what the woman said to her so I insisted, "What did she say?"

"We were in her car and she began to touch me. At first I thought she was just being friendly, I did not completely follow her intention. Then I understood and I liked it. There were not many words between us, it was not verbally explicit but it was explicit physically. After that we saw each other a few more times. It seemed like it was her first experience also. I was twenty-five, something like that, twenty-six and she must have been twenty-two and had a boyfriend. At no point did it occur to me to be a couple with her because it seemed her life was going in another direction. After that I went out with men and my experience with a woman remained like a memory in a box, like a nice memory to say, 'Look!' she laughed. "To take it out of the trunk when I wanted to and remember it and that was it. Then I had a violent experience with the next man I went out with, an experience that was very difficult for me to recuperate from."

This last thing she told me made me think that there are women who approach love with another woman and live that moment as a step they take to an unknown place. It is as if they want to explore loving a woman and having a sexual relationship but without intentions to stay living in that experience. Some women try it and then leave but others of us stay because we find it to be a better place.

"I returned from a more traditional and conventional life with a man to try love with a woman because in the end the only gratifying memory that I had was with a woman. I tried through chat rooms and game rooms to see what I could find. I didn't want to meet someone just for a night, a week, or a month when I was drunk. I wanted something more. I met Caro (Carolina) online and we chatted and emailed for a month. She insisted that we meet. I did not have the intention at the time for something serious or overly intense. I was more interested in taking small steps. At first I didn't think my affection for women would be a permanent thing. I still think, even today, that my experiences with women will not be permanent. To me I think of these attractions as something momentary. I like and accept the game for this moment. The thing is that with Caro, it was a game for four years."

"And how did you live that relationship?"

"In reference to what?"

"I reference to your life, to your family. In other words, does your family know?"

"You mean have I told them or not?"

"Yes, about telling them or not. You were in a serious relationship with someone. Didn't you live with your parents at the time?"

"Yes."

Many lesbians have long-term relationships. In general they live alone and do not have to hide it. It is not complicated when a girlfriend wants to stay the night. For women who still have not declared their homosexuality to a family with whom they live, it can become difficult to remain a stable couple. Or sometimes what happens is that the family sees what is happening but does not talk about it. They establish a pact of silence that is difficult to break. These situations typically generate a lot of discomfort.

"How did Carolina fit in the family picture? Did she participate? In what capacity?"

"She was a friend whom they knew and loved. They saw her as that. I went to stay at her house and she at mine. I never said, 'She is my friend.' I never gave her a title. I do not feel that I lied to them. The introduction was: 'Carolina…my dad, my mom.' They imagined 'that'… and I never said anything different. I never said the truth or a lie. They knew her well and her family knew me well. And I did not feel the need to tell. With my ex…boy…well, I do not know what words to call that … idiot, the man who abused me. To live through a violent experience is vivid and particular; it fills your life with many things—with silence, with isolation, with anger and terror. From that relationship I learned that there were things you do not discuss, and that's it. I did not feel the need to confide about it. And Carolina and I both agreed to this. It was her first relationship and my first serious relationship with a woman. We were in a parallel process. Carolina also did not tell her family at first, but at some point she felt the need to talk about it while I did not. She told her mom—she did not live with her mom—she lived with another family member with whom she did not confide. It seems that a lesbian woman who is living with her family is in a much more difficult situation. It makes confiding in her family more difficult.

When Carolina told her mom, her mom did not believe her. She also told others and *they* did not believe her. I think partly because she is very feminine there was a sense of disbelief—that a feminine woman could be a lesbian. You say, 'No!!!! That is a joke. You're messing with me.'"

"Yes. That helps to dispel the myth that women have to be masculine to like other women."

"Exactly. But even for me it was difficult to believe that when she stopped going out with me she continued to go out with other women. Even more, it was terrible to go out with her because other people were hitting on her in front of me. Flowers were always being sent to the house, someone always called. I asked, 'What do you expect me to do in this situation?'" Valeria continued,

"It is an uncomfortable situation to be out with your girl or your woman when all the men whose paths you cross try to seduce either her or you yourself. It is uncomfortable because it puts you in a situation where you feel naked and vulnerable. You can feel pressured to disclose the nature of who you are and the status of your relationship when you really do not want to do so. It is like playing hide-and-seek and being discovered just seconds after beginning to count. It puts you in the dilemma of 'what do I do'? And you begin to think, what do I want her to do? But the truth is most of the time you are better off if you relax and trust your girlfriend.

"Ok, back to you, because I am interviewing you, not Caro. If you want you can give me her email and I can contact her later. But I do think that was interesting, though, the part about people not believing your girlfriend was a lesbian because she is feminine. "You have not told your family yet? You still do not feel it necessary to tell them?"

"No. Not my family. Right now I am telling friends only."

"Your friends. What reactions are you finding? What do they say?"

"All good, nothing."

"Nothing at all?"

"My friends who have known me all my life don't say anything. In fact, one friend met my new girlfriend, Fabi, and told me, 'I adore her. Finally you found someone like us.' I told one friend of mine who has a gay brother and she is so happy; she keeps saying, 'How wonderful! First my brother, now my friend. How great!' She is happy that her brother is not the only one she knows who is gay. Then there are people who I want to tell and I know they will say, 'Oh, I am gay, too!'"

"And why don't you tell them? What is holding you back?"

"Some of my friends and I can be pretty odd. Despite the fact we have known each other for a long time there are some things we never ask each other. When I told them, 'I went out with Caro for four years,' none of them inquired further about the nature of the relationship. They did not ask me anything, so I wonder if the reason is because they, too, have lived some things and not told me."

"When you told people, who was the first friend you told? Do you remember? How did you tell them, did you use a particular word to describe your experience?

"I said, 'You remember Carolina, right?' 'Yes,' she said. 'Well, Carolina and I went out.' After that I do not know what I said, maybe, 'I am not a lesbian'? Or I might have said, "My girlfriend is a lesbian, yes, but I am not. She went out with me, ha-ha. She insisted—it was all her idea, not mine.'"

In listening to Valeria, I feel that she has a certain necessity to escape from her reality, to go round and round to *not* name herself. She has a memorized speech in order to escape labeling herself. In fact up until this point she has only told the story of Carolina, her ex.

"Does your family know?"

"No, they do not know."

"Why don't they know?"

"I live in a religious family, and they would consider my lifestyle dogmatically bad. According to them, homosexuality is not good, just as divorce is not good. My family is not ok with a lot of things that happen in real life. Personally, I think they have a poor interpretation of the scriptures and of the mercy we suppose a good God possesses. In this sense I am calm about it. In fact, as the coordinator of a group of adolescents from a parish church, I try to transmit the idea of a God who does not watch and punish but one who, in the end, understands and accompanies us on our journeys. From my side everything is fine. Even though for me being attracted to a woman is absolutely normal I recognize that the people around me who are religious (including my family and friends) have other ideas about this topic. A lot of my community I met in church"

"When you say 'church,' is it Catholic?"

"Yes, the Catholic Church and some family who belong to the Evangelical Church, the type of people I am absolutely certain would no longer let me see their children, who are my nephews and nieces, if they knew about my sexuality. I fear basically this—not being able to see my nieces and nephews. I could give up my relationship with my parents, even with my brother, but I do not want to give up being able to see my nieces and nephews. That is why I do not tell them. Yes, I would come out in another situation, but not this one. There would have to be another circumstance, for example, living alone."

"To have a kind independence?"

"I have economic independence, but not independence of structure and shelter. In my circumstances, which have to do with the economic needs of my family, living in a neighborhood also complicates things. I do not know many lesbian girls except for those who are completely out and live downtown."

"Would you say that the people who live on the outskirts of town do not come out and define themselves?"

"I am very certain that complicates the situation of coming out for them. I also do not know that many women like myself, but based on what my ex told me, yes, the peculiarity of the neighborhood is quite unique. In your apartment you can vaguely hear what the others are saying. Moving every couple of years when your lease is up causes a sense of rootlessness and lack of connection with the neighbors. Because of this the neighbors often do not know about your life. Having lived in the neighborhood, knowing all the neighbors of my parents, my religious family, I know that if they found out about my sexual preference this would disgust them, a disgust that would affect me a lot. I have a gay friend who lives in a small town and experiences the same situation. It seems that, yes, it does make things a bit more complicated. You can do what you want with your life but when it affects the well-being of your family you think twice. Even when Caro left the house in the morning, although everything was fine, I still looked around to see if the neighbors were snooping and watching because their comments could be very sharp, very cruel."

"Did they make any comments when Caro left your house?"

"Well, they shouted a few things a couple times and I do not know if it was just coincidence."

"Things like what?"

"Well, I remember one time they shouted in front of me. I do not remember very well, luckily, but it was something like, 'Now the lies are showing,' Liars, or something like that, right when she was leaving. I said that they were talking amongst themselves or maybe they were talking about me. You never know. These indirect types of comments do not bother me, but if they get to my parents, that is something else entirely."

I decided to add to the conversation by sharing my experience. "Ok, I am going to tell you a story. I also live on the periphery. The difference is that I live alone and am not from this city. Because of this, I share a little bit in common with your story, of protecting the family while I had a girlfriend. When we separated I figured that no one had known, but really I realized that everyone knows about my life. Now I feel liberated and if they want to know, let them know."

"And how did they know if you had not told them?"

"Because people are not stupid, that is why. Because they see how people act and put two and two together. We moved together to a house and when we separated my neighbor who was also going through a breakup at the same time, came over and said, 'Alfredo left, we are separated.' 'Yeah? Leila also left to go to her own house,' I said. 'Well, Negra, something better will come along, whatever you need, if you want to talk, come on over. We are both in the same situation.'"

Valeria laughed a lot as she continued to tell her story. I think she did not even consider that people can draw conclusions on their own and do not need words or declarations to know when someone is a lesbian. It is as if she thought that by avoiding naming herself and letting others name her she would rid herself of the desires to be with a woman, that this would remove the 'pretty memories' and keep them hidden in a box for when she wanted to relive them."

I sensed that Valeria was bothered a bit, that what she was feeling at the moment could not be put into words so I decided to move on to another question. It was not my purpose to judge or criticize the lives of the women I interviewed in relation to how they lived their lives or to judge their choices about how to come out (or not come out) of the closet. Everyone comes out of the closet when it is time to come out, not sooner, not later. Everyone knows her moment. I skip to another question, which is perhaps the most frequent one that homosexuals ask of themselves and the scientific community asks of us.

"Do you consider homosexuality to be a choice or an inherent part of you, perhaps with a genetic component?

"It is a choice."

"It is a choice? You chose?"

"No, the women chose for me."

It seems almost impossible for Valeria to take responsibility for her actions. She will not admit, at least for now, that she chooses the women with whom she connects romantically.

"In other words, you choose to be homosexual, that you like women?"

"I do not know if I am. I still do not define myself as homosexual, why are you forcing me to?"

"My intention is not to pressure you, only to try and understand what you are saying."

"There is a sense that sometimes your life itself condemns you, but, what do I know? Yes, it is a choice. But the other day there was a scientific report that said that the way the brain is formed in the womb both structurally and hormonally influences behavior. I am going to tell this to my dad, tell him that my choice to love women is not entirely my fault."

My idea with asking specific questions was to reflect on the origins of sexual orientation. I think there used to be a general idea among those who are not homosexual that one chooses to be homosexual. Personally, I think that nothing could be farther from the truth. We do not choose to like women and go against everything that society believes, but rather it is a question of what we feel. Even more, to me it is something visceral that comes from the chakra solar plexus. As Valeria is a woman with a good sense of humor, I allow myself to suggest that she paper her house with the article she read as a way to tell her parents of her sexuality without having to say a word.

She talks about, in a joking tone, the unavoidable guilt she sometimes feels because she is different and I remember my own regrets when I first defined myself. At that time I asked myself, "Can we talk about blame in reference to the decision to live openly and freely with our sexuality? Can we talk about our responsibilities to ourselves and others?" These are recurring questions that we ask ourselves, or at least that I asked myself when I defined myself.

I distrust the scientific research in its eagerness to answer questions about things that are seen as abnormal. I no longer ask myself why I like women, nor do I need to explain why I feel attracted to them or why I feel more pleasure in bed with them. I simply live it.

The conversation continues and at this moment I ask Valeria about her first time, her first night of love and sex with a woman.

"How was sex for the first time with a woman?"

"Confusing, because I did not really know what to do, but with a man it was also confusing because I did not know what to do then either."

"And what difference did you find between the first time and other times, if there is a difference?"

"The first time with a man, I felt that he was in charge. The first time with a woman, I felt that we were in equal positions. Many times with a man I felt that his body was too rudimentary, too rustic, too aggressive. The body of a woman feels different—the texture of the skin, the hair, the voice, the absence of facial hair; there is a different texture of love with a woman, a different heat."

Valeria and I are still at the crowded restaurant.

Sitting at one of the tables next to us is a grandmother with her grandson. Valeria looks at the boy and says, "Oh, a boy! How lovely, how appropriate! He is going to hear us talking and be traumatized." Valeria looks at me, anxious to continue, and says, "What else?" I say, "I don't know." "I am confused," she says. "The presence of the boy and the grandmother has taken me out of the conversation and I have to gather my thoughts again."

"Ok, I have another question. Before being with a woman, had you considered having sex with one, or had you never imagined it?"

"No, I had never imagined it, or I had imagined a kiss and nothing more."

"With what word do you prefer to name us?"

She does not allow me to finish and asks, "Or by what word do I feel most offended?" Her quick interruption surprises me, so I ask, "How did you know the question?" I had forgotten that she was a fan of my blog, and that she had come to it because of the need to meet other women who were experiencing the same moments or sensations that she was. Maybe my blog had been a good resource for her after discovering the existence of others like herself. Because in the end no one wants to be the black sheep of the family and even less the black sheep of all of society. Maybe it was a coincidence, or maybe not, but in the moment that I was editing the interview, my phone rang and it was Valeria asking about a group of women who wanted to get together. She continued, "In the end I never spoke to anyone about this." She felt a need to say it, to take it apart, to understand it, recognize it and identify with others. To know that she was and is not alone in this heteronormative world, that there is no reason to mimic the heteronormative either. She needs someone who can help her to feel so she can live her sexuality free from needless complexities or guilt.

Valeria answers my question,

"The word I am most offended by is *torta—la mesa dulce*. That is the worst. But even 'homosexual' is offensive to me."

"Why does "homosexual" offend you?"

"I don't know. Why do we have to label sexual orientation if it is one choice among many? To me it unnecessary. I also do not like the word, "*tortillera.*" It is ugly. The only word that I like is "gay." Because it is asexual. Isn't it for both male and female homosexuals?"

"Yes, yes, we understand it because it comes from English, and is a name applied to both sexes."

I had already finished with the questions but she insisted on knowing what story I found the most interesting among the ones I had heard so far.

I told Valeria, "I remember one of the first interviews I did that surprised me was with a woman who told me she needed to connect the different parts of herself. It seemed she could not separate her sexual choice apart from her profession and her meet-up groups because she played all of these different roles: a lesbian, social communicator, daughter, sister, etc., at the same time. Did you know social workers and those who work in the field of communications make up a large percentage of the lesbian population?"

"Really? That must mean something."

"And that is what impressed me the most about this question of words, to be able to articulate your feelings and express them, to name what you like."

"Well, I am also a communicator and I learned that it is not always easy to define and communicate your experience. It is almost too personal."

"How is that?"

"With what you said earlier about violence. There are some women who have experienced sex with a man as violent, just from the sheer reality of how a man is sexual versus how women are sexual with each other. They are different experiences and sometimes there are not adequate words to describe the difference. Maybe it's a little crazy to even try and describe the differences"

"No, I think it's ok. You have said, 'I do not like labels' but we have a need to name things, people, desires, because if we do not name them, if we do not name ourselves, we do not exist and are invisible, correct?"

"Yes, everything needs words."

"In the northern part of Argentina, people are very quiet. I do not think that people from the north are as extroverted as those who are from the interior of the country. That does not mean that things do not happen or that feelings do not exist. Things happen all the same. What it means is that people do not talk about their lives, especially non-traditional lives. The fact that someone cannot define something does not mean that it does not exist."

"You have me thinking. I believe in the necessity of naming our experiences and feelings but as soon as you name them, not everyone agrees or understands."

"Exactly. I coordinate a group and try to get the youth to talk, because letting thoughts and feelings out really helps. Keeping feelings and thoughts to yourself does not help. My dad is a very quiet man, but that does not mean he does not have a life. He does not put a lot of words to his life, but he has a life and he lives."

Before turning off the mp3, I agreed with her last comment, but it left me thinking. I realized that there are many people who do not come from extroverted cultures as she said. These cultures, or at least a sizeable part of the population within the culture, do not rely on highly sophisticated methods of verbal communication, but they still live. The populations in the north that she referred to in fact rely on other forms of communication and expression such as rituals that are reproduced and transmitted from one generation to another. In a very concrete way these rituals serve the same purpose as verbal language by identifying and naming important details.

To break this pattern of what has been a kind of "historical silence" surrounding minority sexualities, I have felt the need to name myself, to speak out. Very recently I realized that my entire life I had been made to be quiet: "Antonia, be quiet," my mom said and these words repeated in my mind. Today I feel the need to back up my words with my actions. I want both my words and actions to be congruent and to say who I am and what I feel.

Words name us and indicate who we are as social beings within a social context. For many of us the context in which we live, work, study, socialize, play sports, etc. is adverse to us. When we are asked to define ourselves, it can be difficult after we recognize our sexual choice is different from the mainstream. Is it helpful to name ourselves? Is it necessary from a cultural standpoint? What are we fighting against as lesbian and bisexual women when we decide to live what we feel? Is it fear of heteronormativity? Fear of rejection? Fear of the established norm from long ago? Fear of sustaining our choice?

How can we start to validate women who decide to live a different sexuality, who leave behind the stereotype and socially established doctrine in order to feel complete? For me, one way to discover the answers to these questions is through discussion.

In May of this year, in the city of Rosario, Argentina, the first national meeting of lesbian and bisexual women (ENLB) was held.[1] More than 400 women came to attend from different areas of the country and some neighboring countries. An important detail to mention is that there was scarce local participation. When I asked some local lesbian women whom I know, many said they did not go because they do not like the ghettos, others because they did not know about it and some because they were very busy those days.

For two days lesbian women occupied the campus of the engineering school at the university, met in a public space, marched through the streets shouting, "We are lesbians because we like it!" Some were jeering in front of the cathedral. Graffiti was visible saying, "Lesbians everywhere," or, "If Evita were alive she would be a lesbian." These words displayed on the walls were revolutionary proof of our right and desire to be visible. These paintings were done at night before the march. Early the next day the graffiti about Evita was only a memory in photographs and in the minds of those who had been able to see it. If we do not name ourselves we are contributing to the invisibility that society condemns us to.

---

1 Encuentro Nacional de mujeres lesbianas y bisexuales

CHAPTER EIGHT
I Love the "Not Me" Girls

I can remember two moments when I was attracted to women. At twelve years old I was interested in a woman for the first time in my life. She was much older than me—thirty-seven years old and was my teacher. Physically she was ugly but there was something in her personality, her authority that attracted me. At the same time in this moment I did not know what was happening to me because I was so happy when I saw her and I always did things to be able to be near her.

Also I was fascinated by Diana from *Alien Invasion V*—the movement of her hips, the depth of her glance, the tight white suit that showed all of the curves of her body. After that, at sixteen years old, I had my first boyfriend and women shifted to second place, but the attraction remained latent.

I do not remember having fantasies of women at this stage of my life, but yes, I can remember that when I was fifteen years old my brothers (who are older than me) bought the magazine *Humor* and for the first time in my life I discovered the existence of oral sex. The idea was disgusting to me at the time. Luckily today that feeling is only a memory.

The other stage that I can distinguish was when I was twenty years old. At that time I was interested in a girl who was more accessible to me than my earlier attractions had been because the girl was only a little older than I was. At the time, I was attracted to both men and women who were involved in music. The woman I was attracted to was in a band that played *dark* music and I frequented her shows. What they played was terrible; now I remember it and it makes me laugh. But at that time I loved it.

I confided in a friend of mine about what I was feeling. She did not identify as gay but at the same time she said she also liked a girl because it opened her mind to other possibilities. After that I said, "I like a woman, but it is nothing, because I am not gay."

The girl in the band also had a bass-player (female) friend who identified as gay. She invited the gay bass player to her apartment and decided to have a party there. She invited all of us. "Everyone is welcome." There I met the girl with whom I would have my first lesbian affair. My friend (the one who admitted she liked a girl though wouldn't call herself gay) and I began to talk with one of the girls who lived in the apartment. I remember at that time we always used the phrase, "Nothing to do with us" with the clear intention to differentiate ourselves from any self-identified lesbian. The woman at the party who already accepted herself as lesbian and appeared completely comfortable with her sexual choice, looked at us with sparkling eyes and with a certain implication told us: "I love women who think they are not gay."

That night we went to a club, one that was near the streets Alvear and Salta. It was very important for me to go to this place. It was the first time that I saw two bearded men kiss each other on the lips and for me it was a flash of freedom—a sudden revelation to know that I could be in love with a woman or that a masculine man could fall in love with another identical to him. I felt excitement at the possibility I could live life honestly and with dignity in total and absolute liberty.

It was an intense night, not only because of the kiss between the two masculine men, but because the girl in the band had dazzled me and she looked like Michelle Pfeiffer. At one point in the night a guy took her out to the dance floor but we were also together as two lesbian girlfriends that night. Suddenly she kissed me with an intensity I had never before experienced, with a flavor in the mouth of more pleasure, a pleasure that filled and burned my body, my essence. The sensation was wild and brand new and I wanted more with the desire to follow the ecstasy to the doors of heaven. I wanted to stay there and dive into the new heaven of discovering love at the hands of a woman. Up until that time, the moment of that first kiss, the territory in front of me had been forbidden and hindered by my ego and social conventions.

A lot of time passed between that first, exhilarating kiss before I actually made love with a woman. I needed time to process the myriad of new sensations. Waves of intensity came and went like waves in the ocean. All of this seduced me immensely. I was filled with life.

I came and went from the arms of a man to the arms of a woman in the process of trying to define myself. I did not yet identify as gay, but I gradually became more open and accustomed to the possibility. There was no question I had liked making love to a woman. To me it seemed as if I had hallucinated between her legs, touching heaven with my hands. I had explored an unmeasured pleasure that was proven in every moan that escaped our mouths.

To me it was complicated to be gay at that time. I questioned whether it was worth it. If I was not in love, or if it drove me crazy to be with a woman, better to not tell it, better to keep it as a beautiful secret.

Sometimes I think my decision to be with another woman was based simply on the fact I experienced more pleasure that way. On the other hand, if I found a man with whom I felt love and excitement, I would not deny the possibility to live that experience as well. I do not know how to define my life for all times and for all occasions. It is not as if I am afraid to say "I am gay. Rather, it is more a question of authenticity; the word "gay" seems inadequate to describe who I truly am. For example, sometimes with many things I do not feel gay. I do not like definitions. I am not dogmatic. I do not like dogma at all, from religions, or from anything else. The important thing is to flow naturally with what you feel in the moment. This changes always. There is a flux, a "permanent state of change" and with the rate that one learns in life. But beyond this, in relation to sexuality, I recognize that I like women; I choose women. I never liked a guy more than a girl, but I do not carry a flag of anything and I also do not deny anything. Say that I am with a man just to *not* say that I am with a girl—never! That also does not work with me; I would prefer to say nothing. I worked for many years in a private institution and no one ever asked me anything and I never said anything. But I never lied. I had no problem with my sexuality at any point in time. I have always believed that I am a person and that who I sleep with is only one detail concerning the whole person that I am.

When you fall in love and live with a woman you become conscious of your sexuality.

After the kiss with the Michelle Pfeiffer look-alike, the following day

I met up with my friends and it was wonderful. This was a group I considered troublemakers—heterosexual couples, and I told them of my kissing a woman in the gay bar. The reaction that came from hearing this news was mixed. Some of my friends were somewhat dismissive and told me that if I went to a straight bar (instead of a gay bar) I would have hooked up with a man, but since we were in a gay bar, of course I hooked up with a girl. One of the girls cried about the kiss I shared with a woman. Everyone took a side about what had happened. Some were in favor, some were dismayed, and others thought what happened was awesome.

Looking back, I do not know that there is a particular date or a moment when I can say, "That was my coming out." I think that moment was with my first girlfriend, who in reality was the third girl I had kissed. The first was the woman who looked like Michelle Pfeiffer and the second was a classmate from university who also did not identify as gay, as far as I know. She was very much in love with me but when it came to sex she got scared. I was into her but evidently I was not in love with her because I did not want to be in an exclusive relationship with her. She was very upset when I did not want to be with her anymore. I did not even tell her; I avoided her. But I think the real truth was that I did not really click with her. I also was still working on defining myself. There were certain previous experiences in my life that had prepared me to accept myself as I am. One of these experiences was when, at nineteen or twenty years old, my dad got cancer. At the time I was living with him and my mom. When my dad got sick, it was terrible. On top of his illness, my life was terrible because I felt that I was twenty years old, alone, had never been in love with anyone and I did not know if I liked men or women. And my dad was sick and I needed to care for him like in *Water for Chocolate*[1] because I am the third and youngest. Then I started therapy and within the year I left my parents' house to live with a friend. This was the first important move of my life. I was able to detach from my parents and feel that I could have my own life away from them, apart from their guardianship and felt that this could happen independently of getting married to a man. Until that moment in my experience and learning I thought I had to get married and have kids before I could leave my house. At the time I saw myself so far from that. Luckily I escaped from that heterosexual mandate.

At one time in my life I had a fantasy to go live in Paris (I had read

---

1 *Como Agua para Chocolate, 1989 by Laura Esquivel*

Cortazar). I studied the Humanities and thought that my life would be wonderful in the Barrio Latino. When I went to live on my own I realized that I could live like I wanted to without having to move to Paris. It was wonderful; I rented an apartment downtown with a friend. My friends came over and we had parties; there were awesome gatherings. It was everything that I had imagined Paris would be, but in my own house, so it was fantastic.

The second big step I took was to meet my first girlfriend. I was finally able to be with a woman as part of a couple.

After I had been dating a girl and really in love with a woman for the first time, I could define for myself my experience and what I felt. I could say from then on that I was a woman in love with a woman and was not afraid to say it openly. But in this moment of first approximation to the lesbian world, I said it first and came out first to my lifelong friends, the same friends who, years before, had been present for my first marvelous kiss with Michelle Pfeiffer's twin.

Many years later, having been dating women for a while, I felt ready to talk to my mom (years after my father's death). Well, I say that I felt ready to tell my mom because my mom started to have a conversation with my girlfriend at the time, to ask her, "And you two, what are you?" So I felt I did not have any other choice but to go talk to her. At the time we also talked about my dad and what he had suspected about my sexuality.

The conversation was funny at one point because I remember I had told my mom that I had been with both men and women. "Oh, good," she breathed out in relief, touching her chest. It was funny. I guess it gave her some assurance to know I had tried sex with a man.

At that moment I only let her know that I had tried sex with both genders and she stopped worrying a little about the topic, but years after that in a different talk I told her, "I am gay." It was necessary to clarify it, not so much for her as for me. I needed to clarify it openly, to not leave any doubts, even though it was difficult for me to name myself.

Everyone is different and you cannot say that one is born gay or becomes gay. It seems to me that there are people who are born with a determined sexual orientation and feel that they have been that way since birth. But I think that for some of the population, yes, it is a choice and believe there have been times when someone has chosen to be gay out of rebellion. When I think of these things I say to myself, "Dammit…then it is not genuine if you unconsciously are rebelling against something," but despite the lack of consensus, it does seem to me being gay is a choice most of the time.

From my viewpoint, I say if you choose to sleep with a person of the same sex, well, you are choosing to be gay! Let me return to my earlier comments where I said that I do not personally feel that I am gay. I mean this seriously and it is not to deny my sexuality. I do not deny my sexuality at all. For me it is more an issue of exclusivity and dogma where people define themselves based on purely social affiliations, or the *ghetto*, if that makes sense. For me, to go to a gay club exclusively for women seems horrible, *horrible*. To be at a meet-up with thirty gay women seems horrible. For me I nurture human relations with all types of people. I am not always around all gay people. I do not need for there to be another gay person around me to feel good about myself. The majority of my friends are heterosexuals, couples who have children, and I share ten thousand things from conversations about music or anything.

The first night of love with a woman was great because I was super in love and she was too. But I arrived at that point in my life through a gradual process. I do not remember one, sudden "Aha!" moment the first time of anything. My first girlfriend was special because she had not been with anyone before (of either sex) and she was eighteen years old. She had never kissed a man or a woman. Everything was new and although I had also never been with anyone (sexually) I still did have more experience with romance. But it took much patience. First it was taking off the shirts because we did not take them off until after things started happening. Everything moved very slowly that first time. In the two years that we were together she never had an orgasm. And for me it was very frustrating and one of the reasons that I left her even though I feel guilty about it. Now that I remember it, I was very frustrated. We did everything sexually but when the moment of climax arrived and she never climaxed, it was very unsatisfying. Evidently it was a trait particular to this person because every woman I have been with since did not have this problem.

I still have fond memories of her and the times we were together, despite the problems with orgasms. I have other fond memories from that time in my life as well.

Luis Eduardo Aute has a very pretty song that awoke in me an indescribable sensation when I heard it at twenty years old, when evidently I was repressing my choice to love a woman.

There are venomous women, there are fatal women,
There are women who go into love as if going to work,
There are women of ice,
Women of fire,
There are women who dream of trains filled with soldiers,
There are women who say yes when they say no,
There are women who search for desire and find piety,
There are women who find themselves pursued for their loneliness,
There are women who begin a war by declaring peace,
There are woman who are capable of making me lose my reason.
Fatal women, fatal women.

At that moment I knew the existence of all of these women. I felt happy and seduced by them (unconsciously). I also knew that these women were resolute and determined to love women, and that they welcomed and embraced their truth with the same smile that they brought to love. Today, I can complete this pretty song:

There are women who desire to love,
We are women prepared to fight,
We are women willing to lose in order to win freedom,
We are women who decide when to say no,
Now I know that there are women who dream of boats filled with women,
Sirens of the brown river.[2]

We are women like all women in search of love. We are women different from those described by Aute who come to love declaring a cultural war, a war that is almost always verbal against all that is established, questioning the archaic and reproductive models of the patriarchal society.

The good news is that it is not necessary to go far because love is always right around the corner.

---

2 Rio Parana

CHAPTER NINE

Escaping the Heteronormative Obligation Is a Beautiful Affirmation for Women

The next woman who shared her story had grown up in the Dominican Republic. She spoke of the unique challenges she faced in coming out in her country. Later she moved to Argentina and more places abroad after that. Her name is Yuderski, and she has taken an activist lifestyle in the lesbian community internationally.

"How and when did you realize that you were attracted to women? In other words, when were you conscious of this?"

"I think that I became conscious of my feelings toward women with my introduction to feminism. In one of my essays that I published, I connected my personal story with the political. I cannot talk about feminism without a story about lesbians at the same time. At twenty years old, almost twenty-one, I was almost finished with my studies in psychology at the university. My life was fairly stable and things were going really well. As I was about to finish my degree, I ended up taking an optional class called "Gender Roles." Now I sometimes ask myself how I ended up taking that class, because really I had no idea what I was getting into or what I might learn. I was always very rebellious, very masculine since I was young, but really I had no idea what feminism was about. After taking the class my life changed completely. It turned out that the professor was a lesbian, a lesbian feminist and a member of a very important feminist group in the Dominican Republic during the 1980's and 1990's. I took the class at the end of 1987. I became her best student and she gave me literature and extracurricular readings to study. We saw each other all of the time. She still had not told me she was gay but she gradually incorporated feminist viewpoints and ideas into class discussions. Some of the discussions resulted in consternation within the group but I admired the feminist philosophies I was learning about and looked forward to talking about these topics. It didn't matter to me that some of the ideas were considered controversial at the time. Through taking the class I discovered a world that I had not known before and one day when the professor and I were alone she told me that she had lesbian friends. I asked her, 'What is that?' 'Lesbians are women who love women', she responded. 'You met them here, here in Dominica?' I asked. I did not believe they existed in my country. 'Yes, my friends are from Dominica,' she answered. 'But are they your *friends?*' I insisted, still in disbelief. 'Yes they are my friends.' 'Wow, how lovely!' I said. And since then my life turned around, a total shift. I became a feminist at the same time I first understood about lesbian women loving women. "I did not and cannot separate the two concepts from each other. For me they are connected."

"In other words you cannot think of lesbians without feminism?"

"Or feminism without lesbians. For me the two came together at the same time. But perhaps not ironically, I also loved men. Actually I am certain that I am bisexual, but I choose to be with women based on my politics and affection."

"Do you define yourself as bisexual?"

"No, I define myself as a lesbian because it is the life that I choose and the word, "lesbian" seems more authentic to me, not because I do not like men. At one point I just decided I do not want to develop and explore heterosexual relationships; I am not interested. In the past I have been with and loved men. In fact I have a fifteen year old daughter. After she was born I had a lesbian relationship. At that time I actively called myself bisexual, but then I decided to build a life with women. I would say the political factors carry a great deal of weight in my choices: 'The personal is also political.' Maybe if I were in a different environment I could fall in love with a man, but I don't really know. It has been a long time since I have been with a man. Physically or sexually there would be no problem; I am not the type of lesbian that would not touch a man. I know there are lesbians who have never loved a man, but I have. Anyway, I have been in the world of women for a long time, and this is the world where I prefer to give my affections."

"Very conscious."

"Yes, very conscious, but unconscious as well. It is the world to which I have been drawn and the world where I choose to live my life."

"You told me that you became conscious of the capacity of women to love women through your professor. I imagine that after that not much time passed before you fell in love with a woman?"

"The first woman I loved was the professor, but nothing happened because the relationship was not appropriate at the time. After that I began to look for ways to be with a woman; I became obsessed with the topic. I went out with a woman for three months and she was the first one I slept with; it was very superficial. Anyway I was very young then and immature. Soon after that I had some boyfriends, some girlfriends, and then I met a girl who became the first woman I would fall in love with. I met her in a gay bar where the professor's group went. Once a month there was a lesbian dance night. My professor took me to the dance and I was infatuated and excited to be going with her. (There were several of us who wanted to be with her and were competing for her affections). The woman that I eventually fell in love with was the first girl who approached me that night and tried to get with me. I did not even give her the time of day. Then about a year later I met her again but this time I didn't blow her off. We began to meet up more frequently and I ended up falling completely in love with her. We had a few breakups due to some flings that I had and then I would go away with someone else for a while. She and I were together a total of four years. It was the first powerful relationship that I had with a woman, living together and everything. I had left my house for her."

"When you fell in love with a woman, did you tell your family? Were you able to share your feelings soon after? How was it?"

"I left my house because my mom found a letter that this girl had written me (Marisol was her name) and my mom called me and asked, "What is this?" So I told her, "Yes," that I had fallen in love with a woman. Later I wrote her a letter of about ten pages, something of a feminist manifesto."

"You wrote this letter to your mom?"

"Yes. In the letter I told her that she did not know what it meant to break away from all of the taboos, taboos that put limits on women and their sexuality. Well, it was a feminist manifesto about compulsory heterosexuality and how I felt it was necessary to break free from it, that if she had dared she would not have suffered so much from what my father had done to her. Blah, blah, blah, and that I was happy. My mom stopped talking to me for a while after that but later we picked back up with our relationship, on and off. After I had my first lesbian relationship, I started a relationship with the father of my daughter and I later got pregnant."

"How old were you then?"

"I was twenty-six. Soon after I had my daughter. My mom was so happy with me! I guess she thought that I had converted back. She was happy that her daughter had returned to the fold, to the right path. When my daughter was a year old I separated from her father and began a relationship with a woman with whom I raised my daughter. This relationship lasted for six years. Because I was with a woman again my relationship with my mom turned bad once again. The first thing she said when she found out was, 'Why are you doing this to me?' And to 'not let anyone else find out, what an embarrassment, what will everyone say?' After she realized that she was not going to be able to do anything to change me, she said, 'You are my daughter. I love you always. But the condition is that your life stays outside of this house, nothing inside the house.' That was how I continued my life of lesbian feminist activism on an island like the Dominican Republic while at the same time denying it to everyone in my family except for my mother."

"How did that make you feel? How did you handle it?"

"No one brought up the topic. They did not even ask if I was going to get married; they knew I would not. It was obvious to me that everyone knew, but the topic was avoided."

"In other words, you made your choice, you had an active role in society, but in your house you were not allowed to talk about it."

"Yes, the topic of lesbians or feminism was not discussed in the house. It was terrible. For a long time I did not have a relationship with my family. I picked up my relationship again with them when I came to live in Argentina. At that point they were so far away I felt it was safer to reconnect with them. Before I had moved to Argentina when I tried to have a relationship with them it was almost like finding myself in an alternate reality. I felt alienated from them and avoided the topic of my identity. The entire situation was terrible and schizophrenic—a public activist who at the same time could not discuss the topic at home."

"Did it bother you that you could not bring your girlfriend to family gatherings?"

"I took her as a friend. They were never going to recognize her as my girlfriend. I practically gave up on my family life, but with time I have forgiven them a little bit; I have accepted the limitations (theirs) and I continue with my life and my public political activism. I have been on TV, I presented a book that I wrote and published. Of course the alienation from my family affects me but I try to combat it by not staying in the closet and I do not let them usurp my ideals. This is their issue and if they cannot work through it than that is their loss and their problem. Having a long distance relationship with them has been the way to achieve a certain cordiality, at least, to have some type of a relationship despite the distance and accept that this is part of my life's journey and that I have to love and accept myself the way I am. I love my mom and dad very much. To know that there is a taboo topic that we do not touch is difficult, but I continue my life. It does seem that there is always a part left pending, unfinished. But what am I to do? I cannot come to them and say, 'You have to accept this.' They do what they can, right?"

"Ok, who was the first person you told about what was happening to you with women, or that you were in love with a woman?"

"To my friends, the new friends that I made in the lesbian community who were also in the same process. We shared with each other what was happening. I also told my childhood friend."

"And how did your friend react?"

"'Oh! Yuderski! You are always so crazy' Well, anyway, my friend did not reject me outright."

"Maybe she was a little bit shocked?'"

"No, no, I do not think Luci was shocked by what I confided to her. She seemed more concerned that people would think I was odd, somehow, that now I was different and would not fit in with society in an acceptable way. To be truthful, I never did feel that I fit in with people that well. I always felt a little different anyway."

"And with your friend what word did you use to name yourself?"

"I really don't remember. At that time there was a complete rupture in my life. I had a boyfriend. Then I broke up with him and I got rid of some of my other friends. I was able to make new friends with feminists and that is where I stayed. When I connected with Luci again."

"Luci was your childhood friend?"

"Yes. I remember telling her, 'I like women,' or, 'I am going out with women.' Something like that."

"Do you consider homosexuality a free choice or something one is conditioned to?"

"I believe that homosexuality is a socially conditioned and constructed behavior. The notion of choice is based on the idea that there is such a thing as free choice and I believe that free choice does not exist in our society. We are conditioned for many things. In fact I think it is dangerous to think there is this thing called 'free choice' or that being a lesbian in this society is simply a matter of choice, like 'a', 'b', or 'c', because that would mean heterosexuality is also a choice. I believe that heterosexuality is normative and obligatory. It is automatically conditioned and installed on a subjective level. But as every mechanism of social indoctrination has its ruptures, in this case the rupture that breaks through is homosexuality. It is a 'rupture' in the sense that some manifestations and behaviors are revealed despite social conditioning and impositions.

"The unfortunate thing is that many people experience much pain when they discover that they have same sex attractions and find out they like women or that they like men. And it is exactly that, a discovery that includes a sensation of pain. We could say it is an unconscious choice that includes many other factors. There are unconscious or archetypal models which we have had since childhood along with all of our life experience. I think that there is a little bit of everything that influences one's sexual preference, right? There are lesbians who have been that way since three years old and there are women who at forty years old suddenly realize something and say, 'I like women.' For example, Ilse Fuskova, the Argentinian lesbian-feminist, was a grown woman with children before she understood and accepted that she preferred women. In literature we have Adrienne Rich who was older, more or less like Ilse Fuskova, who came into feminism and said, 'I want to love women.' From that moment on she never again was with a man. I do believe sexual orientation is malleable. It could appear at whatever time in life. Some choices seem to be made sooner and come from the unconscious.

If a three year old girl can have a woman as an object of desire it is unconscious. But later on in adulthood, which is how it happened with me, the desire becomes conscious. I think that being a lesbian is a valiant self-actualization, no matter when that actualization comes. To accept yourself as a lesbian is a sign of rebellion and bravery against society and its norms."

Turning to a more direct and explicit question, I asked her, "And how was sex for the first time with a woman?"

"Sex with a woman—fantastic; it was always very good having sex with a woman."

"What about it impacted you most?"

"I am not certain I can give you a satisfactory answer about my first time because I do not remember it that well. I can talk more about what I have learned as I have grown older and what has continued to influence me as an adult lesbian. I consider sexuality to be a construction and that sexuality is also a process. I do not climax now the same as I climaxed when I was twenty years old. The way I have an orgasm now has nothing to do with the way I did at twenty. Now I think about it and I say, 'That was nothing like what I feel now.' This has to do with all of the learning, after all, and also the body in its malleability has learned many things. With each partner, I started to make love differently, learning from each woman. The quality of the experience also depended on me, on how I felt at the time in that moment and on where I seemed to be at in my life in general. For me what I enjoyed the most was the possibility of complete surrender. There is both a spiritual and physical immersion of the flesh, of desire and the senses. But with this came questions of another type as well. The sexual experience was of the flesh but for me it was also spiritual, even if that word might not be the best way to describe it. I love the possibility of complete surrender from both women.

Before being with a woman sexually, had you imagined sex with a woman?"

"Yes, but the fantasies were subtle and something I noticed only on the periphery of my consciousness. I first started to think of being with a woman sexually before I actually knew that there were women called lesbians. Also in my family there was sort of a taboo against even thinking about same sex relationships because I have a second cousin who died of AIDS. Back then we knew little about how AIDS was transmitted or how it could be prevented. Same-sex attractions were viewed (even beyond taboo) as something dangerous. At the time I was aware of different sexualities and different genders, transgender people and homosexuals, but these topics were all considered taboo. The dominant and sanctioned cultural message was the heteronormative model.

The cultural tradition and fate of a woman was emphatically to be 'beside her man,'"

"Subordinate to her man."

"Yes, subordinate. That is why I asked my professor, 'In what country? Are they friends of yours?' I had never imagined these women loving women in my own country, in the Dominican Republic."

I asked Yuderski, "Is there a particular word or words used to talk about lesbians that bother you, if any?"

"A word that bothers me? No, none related to sexuality in and of itself. On the other hand, regarding country of origin and race, I get more aggravated when people draw prejudiced conclusions based on these stereotypes. For example, when it is assumed that someone like me could only be a whore, not that I have anything against hookers, only that I think it is terrible how stereotypes are applied in this sense. The terms are used to put a person down, including in the gay scene, 'I am the Dominican lesbian whore.' Whore and lesbian, even though they are not related, but somehow they get combined like that. So yes, there are words that hurt me a lot, from xenophobia, racism, from the double moral standard that is part of that. But really the names *torta, tortilla*… in Dominica they say '*maricona,*' in Brazil '*zapatao.*' I like all of these names because we take them and reclaim them to use them positively, so it is good."

"Are you saying there is a redefinition of words?"

"Yes, I think that 'whore' hurts me more, even though it does not mean the same thing to all people in all cultures. Many times in history the whore has been the free woman, but the idea of the free woman has also been problematic. In one sense the whore filled the role she was told to fill, which was to serve men; hence the reason the word has a problematic history. "

"So that bothers you. And what word do you use to identify yourself, the one you call yourself daily?"

"I generally call myself a feminist lesbian."

"Does that come from a political position?"

"Yes, of course, totally, my vision of the world, my vision of utopia, the future, the struggle."

"What does visibility mean to you?"

"Visibility supports and validates the continued existence of identity. Visibility is also about inclusion. I think for lesbians, the topic of visibility is a central concern. When *Inadi*, or the *Office of Diversity of Rosario*, says that transgender people are the most marginalized group, they say it because transgender people are much more visibly exposed, especially male-to-female persons who do not pass well. When trans people are physically attacked, this visibility obviously makes them vulnerable. Lesbians are not visible in this way. We blend in.

"Lesbians are not acknowledged. Our identities, most of the time, remain hidden and, therefore, we are considered insignificant. Some lesbians think that by staying hidden they will avoid aggression on the street. But what about the insults and aggression committed against lesbian identity by your own family? That is a form of aggression also, but that aggression is not counted or recognized for what it is: hurtful and dismissive. A physical beating in the street gets noticed. The silent, insulting and dismissive type of aggression from others who invalidate us is not counted. This is what many do not understand, including other political factions within the LGBT community. They often fail to appreciate that the lesbian condition is different from other groups of sexual diversity in significant and important ways. Because of their failure to grasp these differences, various political factions within the LGBT community actually contribute to lesbian invisibility. That is a terrible way to live!"

"Invisible and nonexistent."

"Yes, it is a shitty life for a person who will never be acknowledged and validated for who she is. There are women who will continue to be heterosexual forever. This is what supposedly keeps these women from being beaten up in the street, that everyone sees them as heterosexual and that they do not challenge the social norms. But at the same time, as lesbians, we remain hidden, living parallel lives to heterosexual women yet, most of the time, we are silent. How many lesbians dare to show their face and say, 'Here I am!?'"

Lesbian invisibility is a disgrace for all women because while lesbians continue to be the hidden subject, heterosexual normativity continues to hold itself up as the "only" valid model for a woman to live an authentic life. This version of the facts is 100% wrong and a lie, a lie that does not support the truth of many women. If lesbians are always hidden, this is a huge topic."

"Exactly. I agree with what you are saying. To illustrate my own experience with this problem, I heard from a girl I met at a lesbian support group and she said, 'If I had known that there were more women who loved women, I would have defined myself sooner and the process wouldn't have been nearly as painful.'"

"Is there anything else you would like to add to our discussion before we finish?"

"No, I think I am good with everything we have said. Is there anything else you would like to ask me? When you first told me you were writing this book I said to myself, 'How awesome that she called me,' not for myself, but so I could share my experience with others. I know that my story will resonate with many women. For me being a lesbian is not a burden. On the contrary, it is a lifestyle that I embrace with much pleasure and pride. If called upon to talk about the significance that being a lesbian has for me, I would never tell a story of turmoil, of a life filled with pain. Instead, I would tell of a life filled with much happiness. Living my life as a lesbian has always been about reaffirming my desires, of my 'being-in-the-world' and is about wanting to be happy in the best way possible. That is why I continue to call myself a lesbian. I see that escaping the heteronormative obligation is a beautiful affirmation for women."

As I think about how to best continue this book and weave in all of these wonderful stories, I am reminded of the words of Yudersky, this wonderful Dominican woman. Yudersky is beautiful, sensual and warm. I keep returning to her last words: "Escaping the heteronormative obligation is a beautiful affirmation for women." When I think of her words, I cannot help but feel happy, content and sure of myself. I escaped. In fact, I continue to escape a little bit every day. When I meet a young woman who tells me that she came to terms with her preference for women at a young age, all I can do is feel happy. That is to say, I am happy for her that she escaped more quickly than I did from this mechanism that oppresses us. It is a mechanism that traps us in a pattern of behavior that does not support our best interests or our authentic selves.

The next interview is the story of Gaby who began to discover that she was a lesbian at fifteen years old. At first, like many women who are attracted to other women, she thought, "These feelings will pass." But no, the feelings did not pass, rather they got stronger. The feelings begin as an uninvited and pesky guest at first, only to later become integrated with the rest of her personality. Now she has achieved what she calls a "happy coexistence" with her lesbian identity.

CHAPTER 10

It Will Go Away. I Am Not Going to Tell Anyone about It

"How long did that feeling last, the feeling that your attraction to women would just go away?"

"For an entire year. I told myself, 'I am not going to tell anyone, or I *cannot* tell anyone,'" Gabby answered.

"Why did you think that? Why did you have it in your head you could not tell anyone?"

"First, not because I thought it was bad, necessarily, but because I wasn't sure if my feelings represented the 'real' me, the 'authentic' me. I saw myself as abnormal at first and I didn't want to be seen as abnormal."

"What is normal?"

"At first I thought being 'normal' was the same thing as being 'authentic'. But now I realize they are not the same thing. You can be authentic without fitting in to the heterosexual norm. But at first I did not understand it that way. Authentic to me means that people do what they want with their lives to be happy."

"Is being homosexual and authentic about being happy then for you?"

"Not necessarily."

"But being happy and accepting of your sexual orientation is what is most important, right?"

"I think you have to be comfortable with whom you are but happiness goes beyond mere sexuality. We are social beings as well as sexual beings and almost everyone must come to terms with both. We live in a society that thinks in a certain way and says certain things and in order to not go against the grain we assume certain postures and try to fit in. When you are young no one wants to be rejected by your schoolmates and friends and you do not want them to look at you differently. If you have a sexual orientation that is different from the norm, these differences influence how you behave and how you see yourself."

"Yes, exactly. As we define our sexual identity and discover the natural object of our desire, we want to be chosen and admired. In adolescence we are more self-conscious about these things and they weigh more heavily on us."

"You told me you had said to yourself, 'I am not going to tell anyone,' more or less, for a year."

"Yes, and I was also feeling other things."

"What were those 'other things'?"

Gaby is shy. Something about telling her story bothers her, makes her a bit uncomfortable to talk about it and that is why she stops for a moment even as I insist that she keep going. I tell her that it is safe to share her story with me. After a few minutes she opens up and continues.

"When I hugged my friend I liked it and said, wow, but I also could not allow myself to be overly pushy or aggressive with her. I did not allow myself to explore sexual fantasies about her."

I felt like Gaby said that in an attempt to 'tone down' her sexuality so that I would not consider her a pervert.

I asked her to clarify how it was she could feel a physical attraction toward her girlfriend but not fantasize about her.

"So you are saying that you did not hit on your friend? You did not make an overt pass at her?"

"At first I just hugged her and I imagined nothing more than a simple kiss in my mind."

"Are you saying that you never imagined what it would be like to sleep with a woman?"

"At that time I felt attracted but almost nothing happened."

"It did not seem possible to you?"

"A future did not seem possible, to have a girlfriend, spend the rest of my life with a woman. And also boys liked me, they still like me."

"Do you like boys?"

"Yes, for sex. Nothing else."

"What do you mean? How do you define yourself, lesbian or bisexual?"

"Look, actually, to me sexuality is too complex to be saying 'heterosexual', 'bisexual', 'lesbian', 'homosexual'; it goes much deeper."

"In what way?"

"In how comfortable and authentic you feel about yourself, your attractions, your lover, your ideas, your fantasies … I do not know how to continue."

"I agree with you on the question of labels, because in that way we get boxed in, but what you propose is a free choice of lover and romantic interest, according to who you are attracted to at the time, which could be a man or a woman."

"Actually, sometimes I meet a guy, we get along, I enjoy going to bed with him. There is no problem, but I do not stay the night or have breakfast. I do not feel the desire to stay with a man. It is nothing more than spending an hour and then I leave."

"It is all sexual, then. In other words you do not fall in love with a man?"

"I don't think so."

"The question of choice regarding your sexuality, were you able to discuss it with your family, your friends?"

"Do you want me to go in chronological order?"

"As you wish."

"Well, when I was fifteen or so, I started to talk with a school friend, an odd girl. We did all our school work together."

"Odd in what way?"

"She was not like the rest of my school friends, she was unique and a more pensive person. She had ambitions and goals for the future and a tendency to be a little depressive. I found it far more interesting to talk with her than with friends who wrote me cards saying, 'I love you' or something simple. In one of my many talks with her I told her that I felt attraction for girls and then it all got a little more real. In other words I was talking to a person who did not give a shit what other people thought about their lives. If I told any of my other friends at the time they would have been horrified. They would have shunned me as weird. During this time my friend and I continued to go to school and continued to enjoy each other's conversations. However, we did not always agree on everything, despite the fact that she did not reject me when I told her I was attracted to women.

I was developing my thoughts and viewpoints during that time. My friend was a good listener. I told her that, to me, there was nothing bad about liking women, or if you were a man, to like a man. I am telling you how my beliefs developed in my mind."

"In your head, and in reality?"

"At the time I was still sorting out my ideas. I had not yet had a sexual or explicitly romantic experience with a woman."

"So it was all fantasy?"

"I did not think of these thoughts as fantasies, more like abstractions of myself and I told myself that the thoughts would go away someday or that I definitely could not tell anyone because I would be rejected."

"It was a feeling of rejection from society?"

"Yes, I went home and turned on Channel 99 'Cero Central' and girls kissed and my mom said, 'Ugh, how gross!' So because of my mom's negative reaction and other negative messages, I did not desire to tell the news of my same sex attraction to anyone. Also, I did not see loving another woman, having a same-sex relationship as something that was possible at the time."

"And when did you believe it could be possible?"

"I continued to talk with my friend and tell her about my feelings. I also told her about another girl that I had a crush on."

"Did you tell the new girl that you liked her?"

"Yes, more than that, we hooked up."

"How did you hook up? Sexually? How did that happen?"

"We didn't hook up immediately. It was almost two years after I told her I liked her. Eventually what happened is that one night we went out and when we returned to the house we ended up going to bed. At first we just hugged a lot."

"Was it like a common adolescent relationship?"

"Well, it was different. It was a little more than that."

"Don't you think that there is a finite line between friendly hugs and hugs of attraction?"

"Yes, yes."

"You laid down together and suddenly you were kissing?"

"Yes."

"Without saying anything?"

"Yes. I had already talked to her before about this topic. I had told her I was 'bisexual'. She had also previously confided to me that one day she woke up and thought to herself 'I am bisexual'. It wasn't long after, on a different day, she thought she was a lesbian. And then yet another day, she woke up and said she still liked guys. So at the time her identity was in flux. It didn't keep her from acting on her feelings for women, though, because, that night when we went out and returned to the house we ended up in bed together."

"Was that your first sexual experience with a woman?"

"Sexual, yes, but before that I had already gone out with women. I also had a friend from middle school, 'my best guy friend,' and everyone called him, 'faggot, faggot.' I don't know why. He did not look gay, but sometimes in conversations or when I interacted with him I could see that there were little things. We had spoken many times and one time he said, 'when you are in the dark you do not know if it is a man or woman.' I wanted him to tell me that he was attracted to men so that it would be easier for me to say that I was attracted to women. Then he told me he had already gone out to Refu[1], a gay bar. After that we went out together and I got with a girl. We had sex, but it was completely different from having sex with a man; it was softer. That is actually what I was expecting."

"Does your family know?"

"I told my mom when I was seventeen, a few months after my girlfriend at the time and I had decided to go steady."

"Tell me, how did your mom react?"

"Well, I was getting ready to leave for Refu, and I lied to my mom

1 Refu is a place exclusively for gays. It is called El Refugio, the refuge, because it is a place where gay people can dance and there is no discrimination or maltreatment if they kiss, as does happen in other places.

about where I was going. I told her that I was going someplace else and I felt bad about it. My parents are good people and I felt bad lying to them, especially to my mom."

"Why especially to your mom?"

"Between the ages of fifteen and eighteen, I was depressed. I felt badly, the kind of thing that happens to you when you are unsure of what you want out of life and when you don't know what you want to do. My mom always asked me why I was depressed and what was bothering me and I could never tell her. Well, not that I could not tell her, but that I did not want to share my feelings with her. One day she harassed me so much about it, as if she already knew, that I ended up telling her."

"And what did you tell her? What words did you use?"

"'Mama, I like girls and I am dating one.' 'How old is she?' she asked. 'Fifteen'. She said something like, 'I imagined that. How can she be fifteen?!'"

"What did you feel at that moment?"

"I wanted to disappear, so I left the house at that time and I had no idea how I would come back and eat at my house."

"Were you and your mom alone when you told her?"

"Yes, on a Sunday afternoon."

"Did she tell your dad after that, or does he not know?"

"Yes, he knows. My relationship with my parents was pretty bad for a year and a half after I told them. It was like I had broken the proper etiquette for being a person and a woman, that I had done wrong and they said to me, 'You ruined my life,' something like that, or 'I suffer a lot,' my mom said. But I have come through that time when things were bad and now things are better. My friends come to my house now and my mom knows they are all unique and different, some even strange, and she treats them well anyway. This is a big change from two years ago when I could not even think of bringing a friend home."

"You said that now you do not feel bad. So do you feel good?"

"Yes. When my mom changed her thinking, it changed my father's attitude as well. My parents are older. My father is seventy years old and my mom is sixty-five. They are too old to understand some things but in most of this they are open-minded people. Like a lot of people, they have had their problems in life, but I think they are coming to terms with who I am, with how I choose to express myself. Do you understand me?"

"Yes."

"This is better than therapy!"

"Good, you will have to pay for the session then," I said to her laughingly.

"No, no, I am going to buy the book, many copies. Parents always want their children to be well; they want to know that their kids are doing ok. The truth is, for us to be well they have to accept certain things."

"In your case, your parents not only said the words, 'We want you to do well,' they also acted on those words with genuine acceptance, is that right?"

"Yes, despite the fact it was very difficult in the beginning when I first told them eventually they came to accept me."

"Did you ever ask yourself why you are a lesbian?"

"I asked my psychologist. I went for three years, from sixteen years old to nineteen. The therapy sessions helped me a lot to discern certain things and also helped me to understand people's attitudes. My psychologist was a Freudian. I know that there are other psychologists (or psychiatrists) who disagree with a Freudian approach but to me the insights were helpful. For example, she told me that there are different stages of sexual development and explained to me the meaning of what Freud called the Oedipus complex."

"Did the psychologist help you to better understand why you came to be attracted to women more than men?"

"Yes, obviously."

"Were you waiting for someone to tell you that being attracted to women was ok?"

"Yes, I wanted validation that what I was feeling did not make me a monster, a freak, a horrible person."

"Other than seeing a psychologist, was there anything else you did to make you feel less alone?"

"Yes. One of the things I did was to visit online chat rooms for lesbians. I wanted a connection even if it was…."

"Very far away."

"Yes, so that no one would find out."

"Yes, exactly. Most of us go through that fear of being found out."

"One of the things I discovered when I began to visit online chat rooms was that I could make connections with gay people from all over the world. I found a really awesome page with women from all over Latin America. I also found a girl who wrote to me from Mexico, but later it turned out she was a guy, not transgendered, just a regular heterosexual guy posing as a lesbian. What a dick! I was pissed off at him after that.

"One of the things that helped me to come out to my mom and dad was first being able to talk to different gay and lesbian friends who were going through the same thing. Hearing their stories about how they came out or were coming out to their families and friends helped to break my sense of isolation. Hearing other people's stories gave me strength to feel more comfortable and confident in myself. When you are hiding something, faking something—blah! I did not feel comfortable with anyone! Least of all my own family or friends."

"In other words you did not feel comfortable with leading a double life?"

"No, I did not. Because it was a double life. There is one life that you have in your head, one that you live on the weekends, one life or persona that shows up in chat rooms and the other life that you show other people who are close to you. Living that way was not good. It was not comfortable. Eventually, though, one of the good things that happened was that I started to feel more comfortable with myself, with what was happening. My life began to feel normal. Then I did not give a fuck, I did not care what other people thought."

"And what word do you use to define yourself in relation to this choice, to this object of desire? Do you define yourself with a specific word?"

"Gabriela. That is who I am. I don't know. I am an independent being and obviously when I am on chat I say that I am a lesbian. To define myself was a process. Obviously it was important to relate to other people, go to the psychologist, to think a lot and to live new experiences."

"Well at the moment you defined yourself, did you not choose a word? You said, 'I am Gabriela' and that is your name, but is there another word that you use to define yourself?"

"No."

"Why?"

"Because I find that other words used to define sexual minorities are too general and people are more individual, more specific than that. Let's suppose that you like girls but do not maintain a long-term relationship. These girls pass through your life without commitment and without intention for a permanent relationship. How would you define yourself then? What if you also like to sleep with men? In my opinion there is not one particular word that really fits.

"It is easier and more authentic for me to say, 'I am a girl who loves women, who wants to spend the rest of her life with a woman', and in the process until I find that special woman, these are only experiences."

"I would say this viewpoint is something unique to you. I say that because I am trying to understand if there is any word in particular that defines you. For me words have always had an important weight in my life. In fact, my profession as a writer is not by coincidence, right? I am a social communicator and we work with words from poetry and fiction to journalism, blogging and many other areas. Society itself constructs concepts, ideas, and norms, then reinforces them through discourse, through words. For me to say that I am a lesbian or that I am a dyke holds a lot of weight. And exactly everything we are doing right now is to define the significance of these words and how they are used at the moment. As you said, we live in a social context that is always changing. Yet historically society's use of the word, 'homosexual' has been disparaged; it is a term that has carried negative meanings in the past. In this way I think that sometimes words can hurt worse than a fist."

"For me word usage has to coincide with actions."

"I totally agree. For example there are many people who say, 'I do not have a problem with gays, but when they are showy, it bothers me.'"

"Well, what other people think of as 'showy' may be exactly a part of that person's sensuality or expression of who they are, including their sexuality. When a heterosexual person says something like they don't want gay people to be 'showy' I think they are really saying that sexuality should be black and white, confined to a narrow range of behaviors and expressions, which of course doesn't work for many people. Does that make sense?"

"Yes. Could you explain a little more?"

"For me, it is seen in all of the gray areas. There are the guys who say, 'fucking faggots,' and then go looking for a transgender person, betraying their own duplicity and desires outside the norm."

"Yes, that is part of the sexuality of that person. He could define himself as heterosexual, which is fine, but he is not entirely heterosexual if he is going out looking for a transgender sex partner. If we go by the definition of heterosexual, which is 'a guy who is with girls, and a girl who is with guys,' gay is 'a guy who is with guys.' In this example this guy says, 'Gays are gross,' yet one day he goes looking for a transgender person. Comparing it on a continuum, this guy would be somewhere in the middle, not completely heterosexual or homosexual. It does not seem to me that sexuality can be defined with one word. 'Sexuality' is a combination of many things including physical and romantic attraction to others, social conditioning, how we were raised, our genetics, our experiences, how we are feeling at that very moment and who is or who is not available to us! I think that sexuality goes deeper than these words."

"Which words?"

"I have a hypothesis that when women name themselves as lesbians there is an entire world, an abyss, that opens up from this word and I believe it is associated with the feeling most of us experienced when we first told our moms, 'I like women and I am going out with a woman.' At that moment we wanted the earth to swallow us up. So I do not think it is helpful to name ourselves when the word used to describe us also alienates us from others by proclaiming that we are different. Aren't we all just human beings first and foremost? Why use words that separate and seem to alienate? And for many the words used do not encompass their authentic selves, anyway."

"Do you think that we are born lesbians or we choose to be lesbians?"

"I think that sexual preference is the sum of experiences during one's entire life. I have friends who say, 'Since I was a little kid, I looked at my kindergarten teacher and knew I was attracted to her.' Particularly for me that did not happen, as I was not attracted to a woman when I was a child."

"No?"

"No, that did not happen to me. When I was twelve years old I liked a boy, and I really did like him. I don't know if we are born with our sexual preferences or if we develop our attractions over time. Either or both could be possible.

"Sometimes I enter chat rooms and I ask someone, 'Are you a lesbian? Are you bi?' and she answers, 'I am a lesbian', and a moment later she says, 'but I have never been with a woman.' So in that example the woman knows she is attracted to women but she has not acted on her feelings. This proves you do not have to experience sex with a woman or even to kiss a woman to know that is who you are attracted to.

To be a lesbian in any moment, you can say, 'I am going to be gay, and I will go to a bar and be with a girl.'"

"By going to the bar and being with the girl, does that mean you are a lesbian?"

"Yes, in that moment, I could be a lesbian, but a week from now I could be with a man."

"So are you saying that if a woman feels comfortable being a lesbian, in that moment that is it. It took only that moment of attraction to define herself. It is like you were telling me when you chat with girls who say they are lesbians but have never been with a woman. If they put their attractions into action and feel comfortable and want to continue being with women, then they are lesbians?"

"I do not know if it is really that simple. There are many people who have one homosexual experience then continue living, seemingly without an issue, a heterosexual life."

"Yes, that happened to me once with a woman who broke my heart. This subject is an important philosophical and sociological discussion that I am certain we will not answer in this conversation. Meanwhile, what is your opinion; is it more difficult to maintain a relationship with someone of the same sex than it is to maintain a relationship with someone of the opposite sex?"

"I do not think it is more difficult to be in a same sex relationship, but there are factors that can be more obvious and problematic."

"Which ones?"

"Family and what the neighbors say are two factors. The difficulty also depends on how each person in the relationship reacts to criticisms that come up."

"Is there a word that you react negatively toward in a homosexual relationship in terms of a sexual definition?"

"I think it depends on how the word is used and intended in conversation."

"And which word or words hurt you before?"

"*Torta de mierda (fucking dyke)!*"

"Who said it to you?"

"A male classmate while I was at school."

"How old were you at the time?"

"Seventeen. But it was not just what he said, it was the way that he said the word."

"Anyway, *'torta de mierda'* sounds terrible. If you had to rank words from most to least offensive, could you?"

"*'Tortillera'* is the worst. It is the one least used but that sounds the worst. From there it would be *'torta.'* *'Torta'* is what is used mostly in our own circles. *'Tortillera'* is not often used because it sounds worse."

"Yes, the majority of women I have spoken with so far seem to agree that *'tortillera'* is the word that sounds the worst to them. On the other hand, most of the women I know do not define themselves as lesbians. They define themselves as women who choose other women."

"That is because 'lesbian' does not sound very nice. I prefer to say, 'I am a gay woman,' than to say, 'I am a lesbian. Of course 'gay' is an English word that includes both homosexual men and women. In Spain and Latin America there is a tendency to separate and say 'gay' for a homosexual man and 'lesbian' for a homosexual woman. There is a political group in Spain that is trying to change the word 'lesbian' to *'gayelle,'* which combines English and French."

"How nice."

"I am *gayelle.*"

"When you accepted that you were a lesbian, afterwards you said you did not want to discuss it anymore. These were situations you did not *have* to accept—the idea of being marginalized, invisible or insignif-icant. Everyone deserves to be happy with their choices in life. It is the only rule that I have: 'Be happy with the life you choose, as long as it does not harm anyone else.' The rule becomes a little more complicated when you choose to be something many people may not like or approve of. But despite these factors, I try to accept the different choices and ways of being that people have. When something horrifies me, I try to see it from another point of view."

"You are now talking about a limitation or dilemma that we all have, that is, 'it makes me happy to choose this, but if this choice causes others to be unhappy I will try not to choose it'. Do you agree with the following statement, that 'one does not choose to be homosexual, one simply is'?"

"I think one chooses to live what one feels. At the same time, I do not think we choose to create our feelings, nor do I think we know with any degree of precision where our feelings and preferences come from. So in that regard to be a lesbian is to be part of a beautiful mystery, the mystery that one simply is."

CHAPTER ELEVEN

I Left My Emotionally Sterile Environment and Came Out an Awesome Dyke

"When did you become conscious of the fact you liked women?"

"The question is complicated, partly because today I think being a lesbian is a choice even though I did not always think this way. When I try to tell my story, I ask myself, 'how do I articulate this'? It is not easy for me to describe the essence of what it means for me to be a lesbian. I had to go through a process of discovering myself, or what I now think of as a process of constructing myself as a lesbian. The process has been gradual and my ideas and thoughts have evolved as I have lived my experience. Today I think of my identity as a construction that is part of a larger awareness. This awareness includes the ability to distinguish and set myself apart from all of the ideas and social constructs that have been put into our minds from the beginning. It includes the ability to sift through and reflect on all of the cultural messages that tell us to live and behave in a certain way. To come to terms with who I am, I have had to sort through all of these messages to arrive at a definition that fits who I am and my inner experience."

"So you are saying that who you are as a lesbian has emerged little-by-little?"

"Yes, my identity and self-awareness came in flashes; it did not appear 'all-of-a-sudden' or 'full grown' in and of itself. I do want to ask you, though, before I forget, are the stories women have shared with you similar or are they all different?"

"The stories are all different and that is where their richness lies. The other day I interviewed Yudersky, a woman who grew up in the Dominican Republic. Yudersky has a unique and different viewpoint on the topic of lesbian identity. I have heard from women whose views are quite simple, all the way to women whose views are extraordinarily complex. Some women have talked about the importance of the political to them while others have cared less about political ideas or identity politics. Not all women who love women experience their identity or the process in the same way."

"I think an important part of my story is that when I was very young, eight or nine years old, I was the victim of rape, which was never appropriately recognized or talked about. For me it was rape, but for many years I was not able to process it."

"By a man?"

"I was raped by an unknown person, whom I never saw again. The trauma of the incident had a strong impact on me. Today when I think of it what affected me most was not just the violence of the physical rape, the act itself, but everything that came after it. For example, my family kept quiet and did not speak about it. My family seemed to repress it and went about their lives, almost like it never happened. Ever since the rape I became more withdrawn. I was distrustful of affection, of physical contact. I had withdrawn for many, many years. As I grew older and entered adolescence, I wanted to have an affectionate relationship, to have a hug, a kiss on the forehead. I also started to experience other feelings I had not felt before. One relationship I remember at the time was a friendly relationship with a high school teacher who could have easily been my mother. With the teacher I was at least able to give her a hug."

"Physical contact."

"Exactly. Which for me was revolutionary because I was a very closed person, withdrawn and very surly. At that time I asked myself whether my affectionate feelings toward the teacher were normal. At that stage in my life and in my adolescence I tried to understand myself and my feelings. This was a daunting and unfamiliar process for me. I did not have it figured out. Years later the question of physical contact returned to me, this time with someone my own age."

"With a woman?"

"Yes, a woman again. I did not fully understand what was going on in the relationship. Up until then I had not had any romantic relationships to speak of, no flirting with a person, man or woman, not in puberty, not in adolescence. I suppose partly because of my natural 'surliness,' to put it one way. I wasn't the easiest to get close to. When I first became aware of my attraction to this woman, I was in the process of deciding whether to continue studying for a doctorate in physics. My psychologist at the time had an attitude very much like, 'No, this attraction is nothing. You are friends, it is like that,' a question that left me feeling uneasy with no resolution."

"Did the closeness you felt toward the woman seem strange to you at the time?"

"Now when I think about it the discomfort I experienced strikes me as ridiculous, but back then I did not have the coping mechanisms within myself to sort through whether I liked her in a romantic way or whether we were 'just friends'. I did not even have the normal awareness you would expect to have, for example, to know if she turned me on or not. The discovery of what it means to be turned on was a difficult discovery for me. I had not talked to other people yet to know whether the same thing happened to everyone but for me it was a complicated process. Systematically for a long time, from head-to-toe, I denied it. I denied I felt anything for this woman. I hid the truth, especially from myself until at one moment I could no longer deny my feelings."

"How old were you when you recognized you were hiding from yourself?"

"I first became aware of my denial when I was seventeen with my attraction to the teacher. It is not crystal clear to me, but from that time forward I began to deny my feelings. And more than deny my feelings, I sealed myself off from the possibility of thinking certain thoughts. I finally broke through the gate of denial when I was twenty-nine or thirty years old."

"And what happened at age twenty-nine or thirty? Did you have relationships?"

"No, I did not have any relationships, no affection, no sexual relationships until after the age of thirty. For me it was crucial to accept myself first."

"To stop denying."

"Exactly, to accept that I was a lesbian. It took quite a while before I had my first sexual experience."

"What was that last gate?"

"At that time I was questioning whether I wanted to continue with my physics scholarship. I was seeing a psychologist. I did not get along well with the current psychologist I was seeing. About the same time I began my relationship with Maria Inés, the woman I had been attracted to. At a certain point I had to change therapists. The psychologist said, 'I cannot continue with you. I have to send you to a psychiatrist.' I got very mad. I did not go back to her and I went to see a different psychologist. The first thing the new psychologist said was, 'When you talk about María Inés your little eyes light up.' When I had described my feelings about Maria to the previous psychologist, that psychologist had always minimized the nature and importance of my feelings and said, 'It is very normal that women have these friendly affectionate relationships.'"

"So the previous psychologist denied what was happening to you."

"Yes. To say it in a crude way, I was very horny, very affected yet could not understand my feelings. I could not recognize them for what they were. I had a very intense relationship that had no possibility of becoming intelligible. With this new psychologist I began to talk about the things that made me come alive. More than a year passed of talk, talk, talk. Finally I said, 'It could be that I like women, but until there is proof the situation is ambiguous.' Well, 'the proof' happened and I gave in to the evidence that I liked María Inés."

"The proof was having sex with her?"

"Actually we did not have sex. It was a simulation of kisses, not even actual kisses. Essentially my requirement was this: there must be some humidity, some sexual heat and attraction even if we did not have explicit sex. Facing the overt attraction was the proof. What it meant to me, therefore, was that I must be a lesbian. Since I first came to accept my sexual attraction for Maria Inés, after that I took charge of my identity."

"In other words you were able to define that you liked women, but at the beginning of the process you did not define yourself as a lesbian?"

"Words that I used to call myself were evolving. In the beginning I said, 'I am not homosexual,' in those first months of reflection. Later, I continued constructing that I was a lesbian, a 'dyke' in the more relaxed, slang version. At the same time I was reading about feminism and I started putting a few feminist ideas together that made sense to me. I started to believe that all words and identities are constructions based on both our social and personal experience. So I surmised and concluded that the word 'lesbian' is a construction also.

"How much of your 'lesbian construction' is based on your political views of men and women and a rejection of traditional sex roles?"

"Well, I will say that I would not choose to be in a heterosexual relationship because I believe it is impossible to have a sexual and affectionate relationship with a man and have equality at the same time. I think that the cultural ideology imputed to men is very strong and that the ideology is sexist and patriarchal. That is a tradition where males are dominant and women are told to be subservient. It is not an ideology that reveres equality. I would not be able to view any man who lives in this patriarchal culture as free from a sense of male privilege and entitlement."

"You said that the privilege men hold in society does not allow true affection in relationships (sexual or not) and that there cannot be true equality between men and women."

"Correct. There may be an exception here or there, but not for the majority of men and women. There is no true equality between the sexes. The patriarchal nature of society does not allow for it."

"Do you think that the question of power comes into play between two women in a same sex relationship?"

"I think the balance of power is a factor, but it is more nuanced between two women. It is not that power struggles do not exist; it is just that the playing field is at least level when you eliminate male privilege and entitlement. Neither woman has either male privilege or male entitlement bestowed upon them by the culture at large. So they begin from a very different, more equal starting point. You can never make power invisible, make inequality invisible, but you can lessen its impact by refusing to participate in the heterosexual rituals society has traditionally upheld as the superior models to all other relationships."

"Returning to the question of denial. After you proved to yourself that you were attracted to women and after you accepted yourself, did you begin to think of establishing a relationship with a woman? Did you find anyone with whom you could talk to about your feelings?"

"Yes, when I faced my feelings and accepted them, I had sufficient support from the psychologist I had been seeing."

"At that point did you tell the psychologist that you identified as a lesbian?"

"I no longer remember the exact details of how I told the psychologist, but around that time I began to come out to people, to tell close friends, cousins, sisters. I had the good fortune to be living alone at the time and did not need to share space with family members. In other words, I did not have to hide my life while I was in my own living space. I had my own privacy. Partly because of my living arrangements, then, to come out of the closet did not feel like a huge risk. When I began to share with my family their typical response was, 'We already knew, but *you* did not know it yet.'"

"How did those words make you feel?"

"Good, because I had completed the process of self-acceptance that began with the psychologist, Adriana. She helped me to accept myself and to construct myself with a sense of humor. Adriana did not talk to me as if I had an ailment or a sickness. In addition to my positive therapy experience, I also went through a period of intellectual growth through reading feminist literature. I had been reading other feminists for some time and my dalliance, my flirtations with feminism allowed me to get to know my body. I learned to accept that my body had been violated when I was raped. I came to accept that the rape had not been my fault and that I needed to forgive myself for the violation, to move beyond the incident. In the process, I gained a sense of humor about who I am and an appreciation of what I had been through. I left the old 'emotionally sterile' environment and came out to be one awesome dyke. To me 'dyke' seems like a fun word to call myself and I like the word."

"You said that you told your cousins and sisters that you were a lesbian. Were you able to tell your parents?"

"My parents died when I was quite young. I did not tell my grandfather who raised us. By the time I had begun to define myself, he was already sick and dying. I did not tell him and I had already moved out of his house. I saw him rarely, once or twice a year."

"You did not feel it was necessary to explain your sexual identity to him?"

"No; he was not in good health and I am not sure he would have been able to understand. However, at the university where I worked I felt empowered to come out. I declared myself a lesbian and I participated in the pride marches."

"I think that I read in the magazine '*Bayruyeras*'[1] you came out as a lesbian to your physics class at the university. And how did you feel in that moment? Why did you feel it was necessary to come out in class?"

"Two years ago, a man I work for gave me a book on electricity. The book had illustrations and photographs to explain how similar charges repel each other and opposite charges attract. In the book were two photographs. One photo showed an image of a man and woman hugging. In another photo, two men slapped each other on the ass. This shocked me and I said, 'This is not ok' and I felt that these kinds of images show same sex relationships in a negative light. It is through images like this I think people construct ideas. They construct arguments. These are the tools and weapons of propaganda that the culture gives us. Such images perpetuate a pattern of normality and the mainstream culture always implies it is better to be inside the normative pattern. Sometimes it is clear to see that it is better to be inside the pattern. For example, with good health, this is a preferred pattern and we can see it is best to be inside it. However, with something like sexual identity and preference which can go against the norms it is better to be able to break free of cultural dictates. The images in the book on electricity affected me a lot. The images clearly suggested that the attraction of opposites was the normative and therefore 'preferred' pattern while same-sex attraction was an aberrant pattern and undesirable Since that moment I told myself, 'I have to denounce this majority-culture mandate. It does not fit for all people. In fact, it is a lie for many'. Soon after this there was a gathering of Caribbean lesbians in Chile that I attended and after that I started teaching a class about sexism and heteronormativity. The class focused on how sexism manifests itself in the teaching of physics and science. Many people were interested in the class. That gave me strength and I became committed to 'practice what I preached' in my classes. I made a concerted effort to avoid sexist language and phrases in all discourse, both verbal and written. In class, every effort was made to guard against heteronormative communication, to get students to think, to show them

---

1 An informal street publication known for publicizing about people being loud about their opinions and bringing to light issues that society likes to sweep under the rug.

that better communication was possible, that they did not need sexist and heteronormative conventions to communicate effectively.

The first day I taught the class on sexism, I told the students, 'I am a person working to remove sexist, chauvinist language and denounce these practices'. Every time I expressed myself in class, I grew more explicit."

"While you were teaching the class, did you bring up the idea of *'potencia tortillera' (dyke power)* and how the slogan evolved?"

"*Potencia tortillera*; I am probably not the best person to explain how the term came to be."

"Who created it?"

"The words evolved from an idea to create empowerment and excitement at a women's gathering from the desert women's group called the *Desert Fugitives*. We got together and everyone made a shirt with the inscription, *potencia tortillera*. When we saw the controversy that these words created, how some liked the slogan and how some did not, it made an impact. Later, in talks with friends, we saw how *potencia tortillera* could be more than a simple T-shirt slogan. The words could also act as a catalyst and tool of empowerment for a lot of different groups of lesbian feminists.

"I think we may have already discussed the subject of origins of homosexual desire, but what do you think? Do you think this is something we are born with or is it something we later acquire?"

"At first in no way did I think that women are born lesbian, but now I think, yes, it could be one is born with an innate tendency to be attracted to women. I also think, however, that to be a lesbian is part of a larger social construction. Social influences are unmistakable and can have a powerful influence on our behavior, including sexual behavior. I think every woman who identifies as lesbian comes to terms with her sexual identity and attraction to women in her own unique way. For me, if I had to say which influence I believe is the stronger one (biology or social construction) I would say being attracted to women is not something I was born with. It is a social construction and a choice."

At this point in our conversation, I abruptly changed the subject to something less abstract.

"How was sex with a woman the first time?"

"A little surprising. The sexual part brought up complicated feelings for me. I was still conflicted about my body and the relationship of my body when touched (or touching) others. I had yet to process all of the demons and ghosts from my past due to the rape. My first experience was planned-out. It was designed, not impulsive. Looking back I believe I wanted the experience to be controlled to lessen my feelings of danger and risk. I did not want any unexpected adventures. I was frightened afterwards. I had a naive and poor understanding of my bodily experiences."

"Do you have any lasting impressions from your first experience with another woman?"

"I think I was more impressed by my first kiss with a woman, actually, not the simulated one with María Inés. After my first sexual experience I was no longer surprised. I said to myself, 'I have to have sex', to go through with it no matter what. There was almost a desperate search. I said a little bit jokingly to myself, 'It is my duty to have sex and I have to do it,' and I did it. In no way was it a test. Sometimes I have heard others ask, 'Hey, you tried it, did you like it or not?' In this case it was not a question of, 'If I like it, then I am a lesbian, and if I don't like it then I am not.' I obviously liked sex with women a lot. I was interested in them, I remain interested and I enjoy sexual and romantic experiences with women so that is that. For me there is no turning back. What I am clear about is that I know what I like and don't like. The same thing happens to me with coffee. I drink coffee because I like coffee. Also, I do not smoke because I do not like the bitterness of tobacco.

I did not say this before but I also think being a lesbian is a political choice that goes beyond the person you have sex with or the genitals.

For me to be a lesbian is deeper than sexuality and goes beyond lustful or erotic exchanges. I could not have this kind of exchange with a man or any other person who does not share this same ideological affinity."

"In the years that you were in denial, both your own and that of the first psychologist you saw, did you have sexual fantasies about women?"

"No, I am not much for fantasies. Like most people I masturbated secretly, but during masturbation I did not have sexual fantasies. When I first began to talk about my sexual feelings and attraction toward women with my second therapist, she asked, 'Do you masturbate?' I said, 'yes' but I do not fantasize, nothing more."

"Are there any words used to describe lesbians that bother you? If you can wear a shirt that says 'dyke power,' there is potentially nothing that can piss you off. At least that is my impression."

"I feel a little bothered when people say, 'homosexual' because it is a medicalized word created as a definition by psychologists. In fact when I formerly used the word I used it in that almost clinical sense. To me in the street I hear 'homosexual,' 'gay,' *torta*,' '*tortillera*,' but they do not offend me at all. In general I do not worry about what happens in the street. Yes, heteronormativity offends me and when a man in the street or in the gym asks me out (which has happened) that offends me. It makes me feel uncomfortable. These things bother me, that when a man comes near me he assumes that I am heterosexual and that I am going to give it to him. I think that before anyone assumes anything about someone's sexuality the first question that should be asked is, 'Do you like men? Do you like women?'"

"The word you identify with is 'lesbian,' right?"

"Most of the time I would prefer not to identify with any of these words; they are labels and make me feel limited and frozen in my identity. But for practical purposes I call myself a lesbian, *torta, tortillera*, almost like synonyms, and I use them according to the environment I am in. Of course in my class I am not going to say, 'I am a *tortillera* activist.' Rather, I say 'I am a lesbian activist.' Sometimes the environment I am in requires me to be less provocative than I might feel. Those times I say, 'lesbian' instead of '*torta*'. When you are in front of a group of people you do not know how your word choices will affect others. I don't usually take the time to ask questions such as, 'Which one sounds worse to you: 'I am a lesbian,' or 'I am *tortillera*?'"

"We have talked about a lot of things. But we have not yet discussed 'visibility'. What does visibility mean to you?"

"One of the problems with visibility is something I have already touched on, the fact that in a heteronormative culture, people assume that you are a heterosexual woman and not a lesbian. Because of this societal mandate, you are already invisible. Society would prefer you stay invisible but I rebel against this notion. I am a woman of almost forty but look how I wear my hair? Well, I must seem a little strange, because my hair is cut short like this; I appear butch. In addition to my unique appearance, do they think I have children also? I think visibility is connected to cultural stereotypes and expectations. What does it mean to 'look like a lesbian'? Can you tell, by appearances, who is a lesbian and who is a heterosexual woman? Many times I put an emphasis on the fact that I am forty and have this haircut. I already went through a different phase of combing my bangs in front. I borrowed that style from a TV show. I said I would create my personality from that style but actually I was just following the crowd. For me, ultimately, visibility is about the possibility to break away from heteronormativity.

"Do you think that visibility is necessary to advocate for lesbian rights?"

"Look, I think that it is necessary to break away from heteronormativity by any means possible. I believe lesbian visibility is part of that process. We do not want to be swallowed up inside a hetero-patriarchal regime that does not support our best interests and one with which I disagree on ideological grounds. The situation is similar to how I feel about workers who experience depersonalization, that feeling of being just another cog in the wheel of a system that does not support authenticity. We need visibility to claim our true selves, to resist those who would prefer we disappear. That is the way to, ultimately, assert our rights and make a difference in society."

CHAPTER TWELVE

I Am Alive Today Because
I Decided to Live My Sexuality Openly

I was enjoying a typical Buenos Aires morning, sitting in a corner café close to the *Congreso* (the national congress building in downtown Buenos Aires). A few blocks away, waiting in a coffee shop that practically serves as her office, one of the most visible lesbian women in all of Argentina was waiting for me. She had agreed to talk with me about her life and journeys as a lesbian feminist. I was looking forward to meeting her so that I could include her story in my book.

Ilse Fuskova deserves a great introduction, not because the other women I have talked to do not, but because this woman is a lesbian activist who has had visibility in the media since the 1990's. She was the first Argentinian lesbian to come out on television on the *Mirtha Legrands* show and the first woman to call herself a lesbian feminist activist in our country on such a massive scale. The extensive media coverage she has received has brought attention to Ilse and the things she stands for and believes in. This has allowed thousands to get acquainted with her and the lesbian feminist movement.

Ilse asked me to tell her what words I use to name and describe myself and how I discovered my sexuality.

I told her that since I was young I had renounced the social mandates that obligated women to perform roles such as "housewife" or to be of service almost exclusively to men. I told her about my arguments with my mom, about how my mom had reacted negatively toward the idea of same sex attractions. I also shared with her the pressure I felt to fulfill and submit to familial and tribal expectations and how those expectations did not fit the person I knew myself to be.

I confessed that I had only recently started calling myself a lesbian woman, that I had been on a long introspective journey before I could name myself without blushing and turning red in the face. Many times I felt I was facing an abyss that hung in front of the word, 'lesbian' and that if I used the name to describe myself this abyss would open-up and swallow my entire being including everything I was, am and would ever be. Thankfully, the time in my life when I felt that way did not last forever.

Since I have been able to name myself and call myself a lesbian, I have felt empowered and the power in me is immense. In addition to feeling empowered, I also feel a deep sense of inner peace.

Ilse commented, "You could pass for a heterosexual woman." According to her stories she could pass for a "*paqui*."[1] I presume Ilse said this to me as a complement though at first her comment caught me a little off guard. The two of us enjoyed a friendly chat. For me the conversation was incredible! I could hardly believe I was sitting in front of this icon of feminine homosexuality. I felt a tremendous sense of satisfaction to be able to communicate with a woman of such insight and incredible fortitude.

Our conversation unfolded like this.

I said, "In my family they have not fully accepted my sexuality, but there have been discussions here and there. My family prefers not to talk openly about the topic, but neither do they talk bad about it or question my decision to live openly as a lesbian. It is no longer 'another one of my ideas,' according to my older sister, who was the one who questioned my decision the most. To my family, I always did what I wanted. Because of that very fact I began to ask myself, 'Why not live my sexuality out loud?' I believe the best way to exercise my decision is by loving and enjoying a woman."

Illse replied: "Yes, because our behaviors contain within them important social and political considerations that challenge the current norms."

---

1 Pachyderm is what the homosexual women of the upper class called heterosexual women in the 60's, 70's and 80's and they called themselves the "betters."

"It seems to me that many more social norms are moved by women who choose to be lesbian than by men who choose to be gay. Do you think gay men are more visible?"

"If that is true, I believe it is because gay men are part of the gender that has more power. Visibility is more apparent with those who have power within the system. You see it more with those who believe they have power."

I ask Ilse, "When did you first become aware of the fact you liked women?"

"When I first fell in love with a woman. I had been married for thirty years to a university professor. We had three children who today are in their fifties. We got married for love, but somehow in those thirty years we became misaligned. I think that in this exploitative system we live in, the professional responsibility of being a professor wore him down in a terrible way. We both changed and then we separated."

"How old were you at the time?"

"Fifty-five. I married in 1954, so I was fifty years old, or something like that, when we separated. I lived alone for a little while and then I met a Spanish lesbian activist at a feminist reunion of Caribbean women in Brazil. She represented Argentinian women at the reunion. I was completely taken with her when I met her. She gave a coherent argument backed by revolutionary theory. I fell hopelessly in love with her in a way that I had never been in love with a man. In that moment I discovered my attraction to women. I discovered for the first time that my primary attraction was for another woman. I think that is the only way to realize you are a lesbian, right, to feel that attraction? I grew up in a rather intellectual environment. I always was interested in the works of women—literature, art, revolutionary activism. The feminine figures were always the most important to me, the ones I wanted to learn more about. But I was in denial about physical feelings toward women. I first fell in love with a woman in 1985. The experience really made a mark. I was never again attracted to a man."

"And how did you act on this realization—the recognition that a woman could be a possible partner for you?"

"Well! Two years after my encounter with the Spanish activist, whose name is Empar Pineda and who today is a very important lesbian activist in Spain, I went to live for a few months in Berlin while my oldest son was working on his degree at the university there. I got involved with the German lesbian movement and that adventure was spectacular. To see lesbian activists in the streets, to watch how they cut their hair short and walked with pride made it obvious that they were lesbians. They were wonderful women, dedicated activists who paved a way to escape from compulsory heterosexuality. After my time in Germany I returned to Buenos Aires and I became more involved with lesbian groups in Argentina and in other parts of the world."

"And what group did you get involved with in Buenos Aires at that time?"

"The first group I joined was started by María Odone. Maria was a feminist who came out of the closet after separating from a military man. She had four children. Also at that time there were no photocopiers. When you wanted a copy of a flyer, a brochure or a pamphlet, you had to print your own flyers. Maria Odone was an important figure at the time because she published the first feminist magazine in Argentina called '*Persona.*' There were also two lesbian lawyers who published a magazine called '*Brujas*'. With the help of a group of lesbian friends, I began to publish a magazine called, '*Notebook on the Life of Lesbians.*' We put out seventeen issues. I am trying to reprint and republish the seventeen issues in a book because they were printed more than twenty years ago."

"What did you do after you began to publish the magazine?"

"I fell in love again and had a relationship with an Argentinian woman who was a filmmaker and lived in the United States. During that time I went to live in San Francisco for a year. San Francisco was (and still is) the Mecca for gay and lesbian thought. I loved their attitude: 'Do not hide, be yourself. Make it clear what you believe in."

"I identified with the fierce independence of the gays and lesbians living in San Francisco. My situation was similar. As a single and independent lesbian, now with grown children, I was free and felt absolutely independent. Financially or otherwise I did not depend on anyone. I did not have to work for a boss. I taught English classes and had my own students. For additional income, I did translations. Because of this relative degree of economic freedom I had complete liberty to show who I was. In 1991 Mirtha Legrand, the TV talk show host, invited me to a luncheon. Soon after, she asked me to be a guest on her TV show. That is when I came out publicly as a lesbian. It was a huge audience."

"Did you experience any repercussions from being on her show?"

"Believe it or not, the repercussions were huge. The show's ratings went up dramatically and Mirtha wanted to air the show again the next day. Unfortunately she received letters from Catholic bishops, messages saying that the station's decision to air the program caused irreparable damage to society so obviously the program was not repeated."

"And what did you tell Mirtha that day at the table when you first had lunch with her?"

"I told her that I was a lesbian feminist activist, that I used to be married to a professor and that I had three grown children. Mirtha could not believe that something (or someone) like that existed, a lesbian activist. I explained a little about lesbian politics and feminist theory. I explained how we do not believe in the heteronormative model for life, for society."

"What gave you the courage to go on TV? To come out to so many people, to your entire country and to the world?"

"There was something very strong that drove me to do it, even when my feminist friends told me not to accept the invitation. They were mostly concerned for my welfare, afraid that my being on the show would ruin me or that my story would be used to tell a negative story about lesbians to a public audience. I did have my doubts before I did the show. There were moments thinking about it when I became very tense. Fundamentally, though, I am a strong person and, as I said before, fiercely independent. I knew I had to speak, to tell the world that there are women who are proud to be lesbians. There are situations in life that push you, show you the path that you must take. Today, rethinking it, I believe there are different levels of energy that propel us to do things, the right things. When we follow the path we are meant to live, we transform our lives for the better and, hopefully, the lives of others. Seventeen years have passed and the reaction and acceptance of women has been phenomenal."

"I think that sometimes we think, 'How can I influence others through who I am?'"

"Then I fell profoundly in love with the Spanish woman. Our lives are not only about political theory and public events."

"Of course, then you had combined theory and practice."

"Exactly, I had both things, love *and* theory, plus economic independence, not having to depend on anyone. Not all women have the independence and freedom I have enjoyed. Because of this I feel a special obligation to lesbians whose situations are more difficult."

"Before the feminist conference in Brazil in the mid 1980s, had you already been in contact with feminist groups for a long time?"

"Yes. I had been involved since 1979, for approximately six years. Before that, I was part of a group in Atem where there were lesbians. At the time, though, none of them came out publicly. Interestingly, many women in the group who supported lesbian theory and read a lot about the topic were heterosexual. They called us 'political lesbians'. The important thing was at least they supported women's liberation and the idea all women were free to choose whatever sexual choice we desired."

"What word did you use to name yourself at that time?"

"Lesbian."

"Had you always embraced that word?"

"From the moment I began to understand that I preferred women. For one thing, the things I had read always used the word, 'lesbian'. I was also influenced by Adrienne Rich's expression, 'the lesbian continuum.'"[2]

"What does that mean?"

"That lesbians are everywhere and that there is a 'sisterhood.'"

"Who was the first person you told that you were a lesbian?"

"I actually first came out to the women in my feminist group."

"Do you consider homosexuality to be a choice or a behavior?"

"We used to say homosexuality was a choice but as I have gotten older I cannot honestly say that homosexuality is a matter of choice for everyone. My understanding of the issue is made more complex by the fact I grew up in a leftist environment and culture. It took me a long time to understand and come to terms with my identity. I assume by saying "behavior" you mean biological predisposition? One of my friends, Claudina, is from the little town of Entre Rios. Claudina says she knew she was attracted to women since she was six years old. I do not know the answer to the question. There is no rock-solid scientific proof one way

---

2 This term was created by Adrienne Rich and refers to the continuity of lesbians in history, daily life and in the individual woman's experience toward embracing her own sexuality. The language here tries to open the discussion of women's sexuality to a broader sense, rather than limiting it to clinical or social descriptive terminology. It combats compulsory heterosexuality and established the existence of lesbians.

or the other. In some ways I think it is better for us to say it is a choice because if you say that same-sex attraction is something biological then the heterosexuals who hold the most power in society will invent some pill to be able to exterminate us."

"We don't want to give them the rationale to make these weapons."

"Exactly."

I had yet another important question to ask Ilse. Despite the fact the question was both direct and personal, of course I had to ask it, just as I had asked the other women.

"How was sex for the first time with a woman?"

"Marvelous."

"Do you remember something in particular that impressed you?"

"Well, I had some pretty intense orgasms, much more intense than I had experienced from heterosexual penetration. My orgasms were centered on the clitoris."

"And before you were with a woman sexually, had you imagined the possibility?"

"Yes, I had experienced a sexual fantasy with a woman one other time."

"And how did you react to the fantasy at the time?"

"Completely pleasurable. I discovered masturbation when I was quite young and I thoroughly enjoyed it. My mother caught me in the act once and told me it was dangerous because I could become mentally stunted from it. I never believed her. I ignored her words and continued to enjoy masturbation."

"Are there any words used to represent same sex attraction that are offensive to you?"

"No, I don't think so. The word 'dyke' does not bother me. Did you know that the North American Indians, adopted the word, 'daik' as a prideful word? A word they are not ashamed of? This would be like saying *tortillera* in Argentina yet in Argentina the majority culture does not consider *tortillera* a 'prideful' word, quite the opposite."

"Do you identify with the word 'lesbian?'"

"Actually when I joined *Occident*, the name of a lesbian activist movement, the women in *Occident* preferred the name, 'lesbian'. Historically in Argentina, high class women did not call themselves 'lesbians'.

They preferred the term, 'the *betters'* (they used the English word). There were two terms that were used. A gay woman would be called a *better* and heterosexual women would be referred to as *las paqui* (packyderm, which had less sensibility)."

"In other words a woman was either a 'paqui,' or she was a 'better.'"

"In what years were those words used?"

"In the 1960s, 70s and 80s. Over thirty years ago."

"On the subject of visibility, what does it mean to you?"

"Not hiding yourself, not denying yourself at any moment. Also for women who are able to do so who are not at risk of possible physical abuse or economic harm, for these women to come out as lesbians publicly, to share who they are with the rest of the world."

"You told me earlier that you have three children."

"Yes, two boys and a girl."

"And how did they accept and come to know the Ilse who defines herself as a lesbian?"

"My son who was going to school in Germany thought it was fantastic. My other son studied cinema in Avellaneda and was also accepting. He filmed me on March 8th in the plaza. My daughter, on the other hand, had more difficulty. She considers herself very heterosexual."

"Thank you so much, Ilse, for spending time with me and telling me more about your story. Would you like to add anything else?"

"No, I have already spoken a lot."

"There is one thing, Ilse, that surprised me a lot, not really surprised me, but something you said made me very happy. It was in reference to a lesbian meeting you attended in Rosario."

"Before I went to Rosario and understood I was a lesbian, I first had to separate from my husband. Before leaving him I suffered three bleeding ulcers (I was cured soon after). After the bleeding ulcers I had an infection in my coronary artery. Again, I was treated and cured soon after. The third year I temporarily escaped from my marriage and ran off to Paris with a Uruguayan puppeteer. But I had grabbed hold of this guy as if he were saving me from a certain shipwreck. Then I got sick again. I felt horrendous. I hurt a lot of people and my family, but it was the only way I knew how to do it. To survive. I didn't even last three weeks with the Uruguayan puppeteer when I already wanted to come back home. But he did not want to give me the return ticket he had promised me. I was in a terrible situation, but I realize that episode in some way forced me to break away from the thing that was making me ill. My kids were already grown. Running away actually saved my life. Look, next year I will be eighty. I walk without aid, my body is able, my mind is clear. If I had stayed with a man I would have gotten ill again and who knows if I would still be alive. I do not put all the blame on men. In many cases the system destroys them, the exploitation of holding a high position or a demanding job, the pressure of a career, especially if a man holds a job for which he has no interest. These are terrible systems. How do we change them? I do not know. When I first met the man who would later become my husband, he studied engineering, theater, wrote plays, but after the demands of a family and working all of the time, he suffered and the marriage deteriorated. The situation became untenable."

"One of the other women I spoke with in an earlier interview mentioned something like that. She said, 'If I did not like women I would not be in a love relationship with a man either because the system overtakes a man in such a way that the woman always ends up subservient to him. The system squanders both of their soul.'"

"Yes. A man who has a high position in a company and puts in many years gets fired suddenly once there is a downturn. Then there is no place for him. It is a very cruel system."

Ilse Fuskova[3] is a formidable and visible women for her generation. In her time she was the idol of the movement and surprised many people. When she came out on a TV show, I was seventeen years old and I had no idea what direction my life would take, much less the sexuality I would affirm. At that time I already lived in Rosario but I did not watch that TV show. I do not remember if at that time other shows took the news and replayed it until it was beat to the ground as is common now. I do not think that was the case, however, because I do not remember seeing it explained and repeated.

I met Ilse in the hallways of the engineering school at the First

---

3 Coeditor with Adriana Carrasco of the Cuadernos de Existencia Lesbiana, whose first volume was printed March 8, 1987. In the 90's she joined Gays por los Derechos Civiles with Carlos Jáuregui and was dedicated to the understanding of lesbians, gays, and transgender people to organize the First Lesbian-Gay Pride March on June 1992 (Marcha del Orgullo LGBT de Buenos Aires).

National Meeting of Lesbian and Bisexual Women in 2008. You could say that I was debuting myself as a lesbian, learning with others, asking questions and defining myself. At the time I still blushed when I defined my sexuality to others. I heard Ilse say that she was alive because she had decided to live her sexuality. That is exactly what she had said on the TV show with Mrs. Legrand. She said that because she was a free woman, not depending on anyone, not a husband, not any provider, she could openly protest, shout from the rooftops that she was a women different from the others. She was complete then and still is today. She could say it and also live it. With her saying it she wanted to share that feeling with others. She herself remembers this act as an obligation to her peers and to the other women who listened to her label herself on a far-reaching media space. Some people categorized her as suicidal while others said she was brave.

Is differentiating yourself a way to accept yourself? Or is accepting yourself a way to differentiate yourself? To know who we are and who we love is to exercise our right to be. Many times we do not know how to do this or where to begin. Many times we are asleep until someone wakes us up. On some occasions this awakening is smooth and on other occasions it is abrupt. But generally speaking, more important than *how* the awakening occurs is the benefit of the awakening itself or as Ilse would say, 'it is highly recommended for one's health'. To keep quiet is to slowly eat away at our insides, wear down holes in our bones as if we were zombies.

A long time ago we stopped being sick, fighting with ourselves. The most difficult fight *is* with ourselves because we are each our own worst enemy. Even if others still consider our passion for the same sex to be an illness, the next generation on the way is luckily already free of many of the questions that formerly oppressed and imprisoned us. And here is the good news: A few days ago we celebrated the six year anniversary of gay marriage in Argentina and this brings us a lot of happiness and a desire to continue to be free.

Afterword

Endings are just as difficult as beginnings, revising and scouring through every word, picking out what makes more sense to me, the most frequently mentioned, the things that still resound in my head, the things I most identify with.

In reviewing all these stories, I looked for similarities among them and differences. In the process of writing this book I asked pertinent questions and some questions not so pertinent. I wanted to discover how each one of the participants understood the 'lesbian being'. So I asked how each woman came to establish her own identity and with what words she chose to describe herself.

Do we *need* to name ourselves? To define ourselves? Is it important to say, "I am homosexual?" If so, why should we say it?

One phrase that keeps going through my mind out of all of the women I interviewed was a comment made to me by a Spanish woman who attended a lesbian women's conference. She said, "If I had known that there were more women in the world who felt as I do, accepting myself would have been so much less traumatic and I would have come out sooner."

As for how I got the idea to write this book, one day many years ago I met a girl in a chat room. I asked her, "How did you realize you were gay?" After we talked together we had the idea to write this book. Unfortunately, I lost contact with her, but I continued with the idea and here I am trying to find an ending for this, my first book.

The "why" to write the book was always clear to me: to tell our stories, to name ourselves, to make ourselves visible and show the world our faces. The purpose is to allow ourselves freedom, to claim our right to be normal and walk openly in the street holding hands with our girl so that no one turns to stare at us, horrified.

At the beginning of this journey I was filled with questions for myself. How would this book affect my family? Although they already knew about my sexuality, I was concerned that some of the things I talked about would be disturbing to them or make them uncomfortable to read about. Ultimately, though, I decided this is my story and my book and that I am the one who will tell it.

As I continued my journey with the book, my life became filled with feelings and conversations with others. I went looking for the stories I wanted to include in this book. Not all interviews made it into these pages. There simply was not enough room to tell everyone's story. To those of you who participated and shared your stories, I am grateful for your time and your openness.

Without a doubt these are the echoes and words these women spoke to me, words that have overflowed on my pages and filled my recordings. The freedom and the allure of these confessions are also personal truths claiming a place to rest in this world.

And definitely like that, as happens in every story, the ending surprises us.

For me this book represents a search and a process of self-identity. I went along rediscovering myself as I searched for and conducted the interviews at the same time remembering my own past emotions and coming out story.

With each woman's story I confronted myself, my joys and fears until I stood face-to-face looking at my own reflection in the mirror.

Writing this book has been a journey of similarities and comparisons, differences and sameness. Through our own voices we have examined the construction of a public identity for ourselves and have talked about the importance of our private experience.

We have heard from women who are older and younger women who do not use the word, 'lesbian' to describe themselves because they do not believe the word authentically represents who they are. So they search for other words: *tortitas, potencia tortillera*, etc. and play this word and naming game, always to challenge the established order.

Inside every world there are many sub-worlds and layers. This is certainly true for the lesbian or any woman in love with another woman. The fact we now live in the modern world and are more visible does not do away with the layers of sub-culture or change the complexity of our relationships. In other words, just because you are lesbian and come to terms with your sexual identity does not mean all mysteries in life are solved! Life is still life, after all.

Now when I look back and go through my own story, I see myself in a new light. I am able to feel who and what I am and to avoid the masks I used to wear. Today I feel integrated and whole and I am relieved that I do not have to come out of the closet once again. Although I do not hide who I am, the honest truth is I do not know if *everyone* knows I am gay. Nor do I have any idea how many of the intimate details of my life people generally know about or care to know. I confronted this issue recently (which in a way is about privacy). I was going out one evening when I ran into my sister's neighbor. Among many things, she asked me, "Did you split from Leila for good?" I was a little shocked, "I did not know that you knew," I said to her. In that moment I felt abruptly outed, exposed and out in the open. The difference this time was that I did not feel the sensation of wanting the earth to "swallow me up." I did not feel the same way I felt when I came out in the beginning, filled with fear, my words spoken hurriedly and rushed-through quickly as if in a panic. However, even then, those who really wanted to listen, listened, and so I opened up and let everything out offering my heart with every word.

All of this reminds me of the beginning, the first moments that I wanted to shout from the rooftop that I was in love and happy with a woman, not to challenge anyone's ideas, but to share the happiness that being in love with a woman gave me.

Now I have grown. I feel strong, integrated and fully accepting of who I am and what I feel. I am a woman who chooses other women to love every day with a desire that more woman take control over their sexuality, to love and be loved by other women.

Agradecimientos

Obra editada en el marco del Programa "Sur" de Apoyo a las Traducciones del Ministerio de Relaciones Exteriores y Culto de la República Argentina.

Como siempre en toda creación, y sobre todo al crear o escribir un libro, es una persona o tal vez dos las que escriben, pero detrás de ellas hay una cantidad de personas que alientan y apoyan a todo trabajo creativo. En la edición en español yo me olvide de hacer esta nómina y no quiero que me ocurra lo mismo en esta, y aquí va mi lista de agradecimientos para ambas ediciones.

En primer lugar gracias infinitas a mis padres Francisca y Marcelino por enseñarme sobre la libertad, a mis hermanos y hermana por acompañarme a su manera. A mi compañera de vida Natalia por creer en mí y alentarme. A Yu D´ottavio por la corrección y regalarme el final, a Andrea por hablarle a Katie de la edición en español. A Katie M. Gray por creer y crearlo en la versión en inglés, y dedicarles muchas horas de sus días a gestar este proyecto. Se le fueron muchas mañanas cobijada en cafeterías a la luz del sol y al resplandor de las tardes, pero estaban alimentadas por las infinitas ganas de compartir este libro, cada palabra para liberar a otras de las cárceles imaginarias propias y ajenas.

Escribir es una aventura que parece solitaria, pero en realidad no siempre lo hacemos sola, es por ello también que agradezco a Gloria Torrano por sus correcciones, sus aportes, la transmisión de tranquilidad que me daba en cada acotación, me inspiraba confianza en un territorio que pisaba por vez primera.

A Programa Sur del Ministerio de Relaciones Exteriores y Culto **de la** República Argentina, en especial a sus responsables Lic. Diego Lorenzo y Bernardo Bouquet.

Agradezco también a la Editorial Transgress Press, por confiar en la propuesta y publicar el libro Words of Fire! Women Loving Women in Latin America.

Y a todos aquellos que de alguna manera contribuyeron a la creación y concreción de este libro, que es como un pájaro al viento libre y hermoso en su vuelo.

Antonia Amprino

Acknowledgements

Work published within the framework of "Sur" Translation Support Program of the Ministry of Foreign Affairs and Worship of the Argentine Republic.

It has been a marvelous journey alongside the enlightened and talented author, Antonia Amprino. Thank you for bestowing on me the honor to transform your words from the original Argentinian Spanish to American English and thank you for believing that I could do it, listening to my dream, and letting your child take a path unforeseen by you. I would like to thank all of those who have been supportive of my endeavor and have listened and shared ideas. Thank you to friends and new acquaintances who, upon learning of this translation, jumped aboard the train waiting to take us to the final publication.

I look forward to seeing where this translation will go, who it will inspire, how it will heal more women than I could have dreamed of and ultimately discover what contribution it will make to our English-speaking communities. My wish is that this book unites us while it minimizes any difficulties inherent in our different languages and cultures. We are one people. We are women. We are queer. We are beautiful. Thank you to all who have encouraged me and supported me along this journey, those who read chapters and praised the literature.

I appreciate the numerous New Orleans coffee shops that housed me from the bright hours of the day into the wee hours of the night as I poured my soul into this text. One of the greatest highlights of the process was when Transgress Press agreed to publish the translation. I am truly grateful to Trystan Cotten for the vision for this book and his support of our ambition to make it a great success. Thank you to wonderful editors Hunter Boone and Shelby Zahn who worked on the book. The editing and publishing was paid for by Programa Sur, Department of Cultural Affairs in Argentina, along with logistical support from the Argentinian Consulate in Los Angeles. We are excited and grateful for this show of appreciation and public support for the LGBT community in Argentina. This gives us hope for a better tomorrow. Thank you to all who have been part of this year and all who will accompany this book in the future. May it bring you peace, understanding and hope while also challenging you own thoughts and opinions.

Katie Marguerite Gray